Additional Practice Workbook

ACCELERATED GRADE 7

enVision® Mathematics

SAVVAS

LEARNING COMPANY

ISBN-13:   978-0-7685-6568-3
ISBN-10:   0-7685-6568-5

6   22

Accelerated Grade 7
Topics 1–13

Topic 1 Rational Number Operations

Topic 2 Real Numbers

Topic 3 Analyze and Use Proportional Relationships

Topic 4   **Analyze and Solve Percent Problems**

Topic 5   **Generate Equivalent Expressions**

Topic 6   **Solve Problems Using Equations and Inequalities**

Topic 7 **Analyze and Solve Linear Equations**

Topic 8 **Use Sampling to Draw Inferences About Populations**

Topic 9 **Probability**

Topic 10 **Solve Problems Involving Geometry**

Topic 11 **Congruence and Similarity**

Topic 12 **Understand and Apply the Pythagorean Theorem**

Topic 13 **Solve Problems Involving Surface Area and Volume**

Name: _____

1-1 Additional Practice

In 1–4, write the integer or description that represents the situation.

1. The temperature was −6°F. It rose so that the temperature was 0°F.

   [＿＿＿]° represents the change in temperature.

2. Trevor spent $27 and now has no money left. He had $ [＿＿＿] before his purchase.

3. On Monday, the price of an online movie dropped $3 in the morning and then another $3 that afternoon. The following Monday morning, the price increased by $6. The price of the online movie [＿＿＿] change from Monday morning to the following Monday morning.

4. A scuba diver rose 600 feet to the surface of the water. The integer that represents the diver's position, in feet, with respect to the water's surface before rising is [＿＿＿].

5. A diver is 19 meters below the surface of the water. Use an integer to represent how far the diver will need to travel to reach the surface.

6. An elevator goes up 7 floors and then down 4 floors. What integer represents the change in the floor level?

7. How do you know the opposite of a nonzero integer?

8. Sean is exploring a coral reef 91 feet below sea level and Liz is hiking 91 feet above sea level. Who is farther away from sea level?

9. What must be true about two integers that combine to equal zero?

10. **Reasoning** A golfer's score after playing on Friday was +2. His score for Saturday's round was −5. At the end of his round on Sunday, he was at even par, or 0. What integer represents the change in the golfer's score from the end of his round on Saturday to the end of his round on Sunday? Explain your answer.

11. Which situation can be represented by the opposite of −7?

   Ⓐ You take an elevator down 7 floors.

   Ⓑ You take an elevator up 7 floors.

   Ⓒ The temperature drops 7°C.

   Ⓓ A stock decreases 7 points.

12. A submarine is underwater. Its position is 645 feet below sea level. It rises in the water 100 feet and then descends 100 feet. What integer represents the change in the submarine's position in the water?

13. The amount you pay for a car is not usually the "sticker price," which may be the starting price. The price of a car was reduced by $300 from the sticker price, increased by $900 for additional features, and then reduced by $600 by the dealer. What integer represents the total change in price with respect to the sticker price? Use a number line to represent the change from the sticker price.

14. Carleton answered 53 questions incorrectly on a test. Write two different situations that can be represented by the opposite of −53?

☑ Assessment Practice

15. Select all of the following situations that could be represented by the equation $5 + (−5) = 0$.

   ☐ Your starting account balance is $0, you deposit $5.

   ☐ The temperature rises 5°F, then drops 5°F.

   ☐ The temperature is 0°F, then it drops 5°F.

   ☐ You walk up 5 stairs, then you walk down 5 stairs.

   ☐ You walk up 5 stairs, then you walk up 5 more stairs.

16. Select all of the following situations that could be represented by the opposite of 8.

   ☐ You delete 8 contacts from your cell phone.

   ☐ You deposit $8 into your savings account.

   ☐ The temperature rises 8°F.

   ☐ A plant grows 8 inches taller.

   ☐ You walk down 8 flights of stairs.

Name: _____

1-2 Additional Practice

Leveled Practice In 1–4, write the decimal equivalent for each rational number.

1. $\frac{7}{9}$

2. $\frac{9}{20}$

3. $\frac{1}{18}$

4. $\frac{5}{8}$

5. A recipe calls for $\frac{1}{2}$ cup of milk. Express the number of cups of milk as a decimal.

6. The result of an experiment was $117\frac{151}{200}$ particles per milliliter. Write the decimal equivalent for $117\frac{151}{200}$.

7. Which of these rational numbers is a repeating decimal? Select all that apply.

   ☐ $-0.\overline{347}$

   ☐ 3.611

   ☐ -1.35

   ☐ $2.15\overline{3}$

   ☐ 7.777

8. A bowl weighs $\frac{11}{40}$ pound.

   a. Express this weight as a decimal.

   b. Reasoning Explain how you can find the decimal by thinking of the denominator as a 4 and using mental math.

9. Determine whether each is rational or not rational.

   a. $-12.161616...$

   b. $9.0832748175...$

   c. 49

10. Is $0.040040004...$ a rational number? Explain your reasoning.

11. During a thunderstorm, 143 out of 333 houses lost electrical power.

    a. Write the decimal equivalent for $\frac{143}{333}$.

    b. Use Structure What do you notice about the digits in the decimal equivalent?

12. Write the decimal expansion for each rational number.

    a. $\frac{1}{9}$

    b. $\frac{10}{11}$

    c. $1\frac{5}{27}$

☑ Assessment Practice

13. Select all the fractions that have the same decimal value.

    ☐ $1\frac{1}{3}$

    ☐ $\frac{12}{9}$

    ☐ $\frac{3}{9}$

    ☐ $1\frac{2}{3}$

    ☐ $\frac{4}{3}$

14. The number of hours in 80 minutes is $\frac{80}{60}$. Which statements are true?

    ☐ The number of hours in decimal form is 1.3.

    ☐ The amount of time is a full hour and $\frac{1}{3}$ hour.

    ☐ The number of hours is a terminating decimal.

    ☐ The number of hours is between 1 and 1.35.

    ☐ Dividing 6 by 8 will give the correct decimal value.

Name: _____

1-3 Additional Practice

  PRACTICE TUTORIAL

Leveled Practice For 1–3, use a number line to help find the sum.

1. $4 + (-7)$ is [____] units from 4, in the [____] direction.

Use the number line to find $4 + (-7)$.

2. $-3 + 5$ is [____] units from −3, in the [____] direction.

Use the number line to find $-3 + 5$.

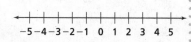

3. $-2 + (-6)$ is [____] units from −2, in the [____] direction.

Use the number line to find $-2 + (-6)$.

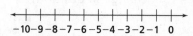

4. In Knoxville, the temperature rises 4° from 4 P.M. to 5 P.M. Then the temperature drops 7° from 5 P.M. to 6 P.M. In Cleveland, the temperature drops 6° from 4 P.M. to 5 P.M. Then the temperature drops 2° from 5 P.M. to 6 P.M.

a. What expression represents the change in temperature for Knoxville?

b. What integer represents the change in temperature for Knoxville?

c. What expression represents the change in temperature for Cleveland?

d. What integer represents the change in temperature for Cleveland?

5. Janet deducted $5 on Monday and another $6 on Tuesday from her savings account. Write an expression that represents the change in her account balance after the deductions. How much money did Janet deduct?

6. Is the statement true? Explain.

$32 + (-17)$ is 17 units from 32, in the positive direction.

7. A squirrel runs 23 feet down a hill to eat an acorn. Then it runs 23 feet up the hill. Write the integer that represents the squirrel's final position with respect to the top of the hill.

8. Mario walks 7 blocks from his home to a restaurant. He then walks back toward home for five blocks, where he stops at a bookstore. How many blocks is Mario from his home?

9. A leatherback sea turtle was swimming at 850 meters below sea level. He went up 165 meters and then descended 165 meters.

a. Draw a number line to show the change in position of the sea turtle from the depth it was swimming.

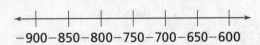

−900−850−800−750−700−650−600

b. What integer represents the sea turtle's change in position?

10. **Higher Order Thinking** Felix spends $150 each month for his gym membership plus $30 each week for a personal trainer. A new gym charges $255 a month, which includes a weekly session with a personal trainer. Would Felix save money by switching to the new gym? Explain.

11. Kirk's goal was to save $300 for a trip. In the first week, Kirk saved $16 from his allowance and $54 from his job. He spent $5 for lunch one day and another $2 on the bus. The second week, Kirk saved $62 and another $41, but spent $2 for the bus and $4 for lunch.

a. How much money did Kirk save in the first week? Use integers to solve.

b. How much money did Kirk save after 2 weeks?

c. If Kirk saves $150 in the third week, but spends $8, will he reach his goal of saving $300? Explain.

✅ Assessment Practice

12. Which statements are true?

☐ An expression for "A diver swims at 14 feet below sea level and then descends another 14 feet" is $14 + (−14)$.

☐ An expression for "Bailey owes $14 and then earns $14" is $−14 + 14$.

☐ An expression for "Gail saves $14 and then spends $14" is $−14 + 14$.

☐ An expression for "Max saves $14 and then spends $14" is $14 + (−14)$.

☐ An expression for "Sera owes $14 and then earns $14" is $−14 + 14$.

Name: _____

Leveled Practice In 1–3, fill in the boxes.

1. What subtraction expression does the number line model show?

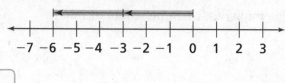

[ ] – [ ]

2. Complete the statement.

   $7 - (-4)$ is [ ] units from 7 in the

   [ ] direction.

3. What is the value of the expression $-8 - (-3)$?

   $-8 - (-3)$

   $= -8$ [ ] 3

   $=$ [ ]

4. Julia is hanging birdhouses on her fence. The first birdhouse is 21 inches to the right of a red fence post. The second birdhouse is 29 inches to the left of the first birdhouse.

   a. Use the number line below to represent this scenario. Let 0 on the number line represent the red fence post.

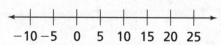

   b. What integer represents the location of the second birdhouse with respect to the red fence post? Write and evaluate an expression.

5. Hank is working in a silver mine 10 feet below the surface. He descends until he reaches a point 57 feet below the surface. How many feet does Hank descend?

6. Nora and Vera are trying to find the difference of $10 - (-3)$. Nora thinks the difference is 7. Vera claims the difference is 13. Who is correct? Explain.

7. An elevator starts at the main floor and goes up 8 floors. It then goes back down 5 floors. What integer represents the elevator's final position with respect to the main floor?

8. The highest temperature ever recorded in Chicago was 105°F, and the lowest was −27°F. Use absolute values to find the difference between the highest and the lowest temperatures.

9. Oliver is 8 feet above the surface of the water. There is a school of fish 10 feet below the surface. A ledge with some seashells is 18 feet below the surface, and even deeper there is a shipwreck 32 feet below the surface.

   a. How many feet will Oliver have to travel to get to the seashells?

   b. How much deeper is the shipwreck than the school of fish?

10. Find the difference.

    $63 - 93$

11. Find the difference.

    $-156 - (-45)$

12. Find the difference.

    $-4 - 5$

13. **Generalize** What is true about the sign of the difference when a positive integer is subtracted from a negative integer?

14. **Higher Order Thinking** Stuart's best golf score is 4 under par, or –4. He wants to beat this score by 3 strokes. With one hole remaining, Stuart is 5 under par, or –5. What must his score be on the last hole to beat his best score? Explain your answer.

✓ Assessment Practice

15. Melissa and Brian are at the base of a mountain. Melissa hikes to a location 27 meters above sea level. Brian hikes to a location 21 meters below sea level.

    a. Write an integer to represent each hiker's location with respect to sea level.

    b. Write an expression to represent the difference of the hikers' altitudes. Evaluate your expression.

    c. Can the integers be subtracted in either order to find the difference? Explain.

1-5 Additional Practice

1. Find the sum of $\frac{2}{3} + \left(-\frac{1}{3}\right)$.

2. Is $-\frac{1}{3} - \frac{4}{5}$ positive, negative, or zero?

3. Find the value of the expression $(-8.6) + 7.2$.

4. Is $\frac{2}{5} - \left(-\frac{5}{6}\right)$ positive, negative, or zero?

5. Use the expression $-\frac{1}{3} - \left(-\frac{5}{12}\right)$.

  a. Which shows an equivalent addition expression?

  Ⓐ $\frac{1}{3} + \frac{5}{12}$ 　　　　Ⓑ $-\frac{1}{3} + \frac{5}{12}$

  Ⓒ $\frac{1}{3} + \left(-\frac{5}{12}\right)$ 　　Ⓓ $-\frac{1}{3} + \left(-\frac{5}{12}\right)$

  b. Model with Math Draw the point on the number line that represents $-\frac{1}{3} - \left(-\frac{5}{12}\right)$.

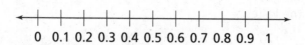

```
0  0.1 0.2 0.3 0.4 0.5 0.6 0.7 0.8 0.9  1
```

  c. Find the value of the expression $-\frac{1}{3} - \left(-\frac{5}{12}\right)$.

6. **Higher Order Thinking** Write an absolute value expression you could use to find the absolute value of $3.1 + (-6.3)$.

7. The temperature one morning was $-4.7°F$ and rose to $11.6°F$ that night. Find the difference in the temperatures.

8. The bottom of a pylon is $3\frac{1}{2}$ yards below the ground. The top of the pylon is $2\frac{1}{2}$ yards above the ground. How tall is the pylon?

9. Manuel climbs a tower from ground level to an elevation of $135\frac{1}{2}$ feet. He then climbs down $27\frac{1}{4}$ feet. How far is Manuel from the ground?

10. When Sam simplified the expression $3.5 - (-4.1)$, she got -0.6. What mistake did Sam likely make when she simplified the expression?

☑ Assessment Practice

11. A researcher in a personal submarine begins at the surface of the ocean. The submarine descends 20.6 meters and then ascends $5\frac{7}{10}$ meters. What is the depth of the personal submarine?

    Ⓐ -26.3 meters

    Ⓑ -14.9 meters

    Ⓒ 14.9 meters

    Ⓓ 26.3 meters

12. Carter hikes from the top of a hill that is $120\frac{2}{3}$ feet above sea level down into a valley that is $43\frac{2}{3}$ feet below sea level. What is the difference in elevation between the top of the hill and the valley?

Name: _____

1-6 Additional Practice

Leveled Practice In 1–2, determine the signs to find each product.

1. Multiply: $5 \cdot (-3)$

The product of a positive and negative

integer is ⬚ .

So, the product of 5 and −3 is ⬚ .

2. Find $(-4) \cdot (-5)$.

The product of two negative integers is

⬚ .

So, the product of −4 and −5 is ⬚ .

---

3. Find the product of 11 and −2.

4. Multiply: $8 \cdot (-7)$

---

5. Find the product: $-3 \cdot (-12)$

6. Multiply: $-7 \cdot 4$

---

7. Four hot air balloons each descend 295 feet per minute for 7 minutes. Find the total change in altitude for all 4 balloons.

8. Mikayla withdraws $20 on 4 different days during a week. Find the total change in her account balance after the withdrawals.

---

9. Which product is greater? $(-9) \cdot (-3)$ or $(-7) \cdot (-2)$? Explain.

10. Use the expression $-13 \cdot 4$.

    a. Find the product.

    b. Generalize Explain why you can find $-13 \cdot (4)$ by finding $4 \cdot (-13)$.

11. **Higher Order Thinking** Three numbers have absolute values of 2, 4, and 9. The product of all the numbers is positive.

    a. Find the product.

    b. Find the different ways to write the signs of the numbers to give a positive product. Tell how many different ways there are in all.

☑ Assessment Practice

12. A number line is shown.

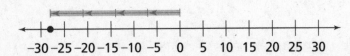

    -30 -25 -20 -15 -10 -5   0   5   10   15   20   25   30

Write a multiplication equation that is represented by the number line.

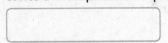

13. An expression is shown.

$4 \cdot (-12)$

Select all equivalent expressions.

- [ ] $-7 \cdot 6$
- [ ] $-12 \cdot 4$
- [ ] $-12 \cdot (-4)$
- [ ] $8 \cdot (-6)$
- [ ] $-3 \cdot 16$

1-7 Additional Practice

Scan for
Multimedia

Leveled Practice In **1–8**, multiply.

1. $-\frac{11}{14} \cdot \left(-\frac{1}{17}\right)$

2. $-2\frac{1}{2} \cdot \left(-1\frac{2}{3}\right)$

3. $-\frac{5}{12} \cdot \frac{5}{8}$

4. $\frac{2}{7} \cdot \left(-\frac{7}{9}\right)$

5. $-0.3 \cdot (-0.27)$

6. $-5.5 \cdot 0.021$

7. $-4\frac{1}{2} \cdot -3\frac{3}{4}$

8. $7.75 \cdot \left(-1\frac{2}{3}\right)$

9. Annalise withdraws $22.50 each day from her account for a week.
How can you represent the change in the account for the week?

10. Kyle incorrectly says that the product of $-\left(-\frac{6}{7}\right) \cdot \left(-\frac{1}{11}\right)$ is $\frac{6}{77}$.

   a. What is the correct product?

   b. What was Kyle's likely error?

11. After a recycling awareness program, the number of tons of recyclable material taken to the landfill is reduced by $13\frac{7}{10}$ tons per month. Represent the total change in the tons of recyclable material taken to the landfill after 7 months resulting from the awareness program. Show your work.

12. **Higher Order Thinking** Place these products in order from least to greatest.

$$5\frac{5}{7} \cdot 5\frac{5}{7} \qquad 4\frac{5}{7} \cdot \left(-6\frac{5}{7}\right) \qquad -7\frac{1}{7} \cdot \left(-4\frac{4}{5}\right)$$

✅ Assessment Practice

13. Town A has an elevation of -13 feet. Town B has an elevation 7 times lower. Write an equation that represents the elevation of Town B.

14. Select all the situations that could be represented by the expression $40 \cdot (-18)$.

☐ A hot air balloon descends 18 inches per a second for 40 seconds.

☐ A hot air balloon ascends 40 inches per a second for 18 seconds.

☐ Tray withdraws $18 from his checking account once a week for 40 weeks.

☐ Suzanne deposits $18 into her savings account once a week for 40 weeks.

☐ Morty withdraws $40 from his checking account once a month for 18 months.

1-8 Additional Practice

1. Classify the quotient of $-35 \div -5$ as positive or negative.

2. Find the quotient of $\frac{-36}{-6}$.

3. Evaluate and order each quotient from least to greatest. Identify any expressions that are undefined.

$$-30 \div 6 \qquad 0 \div (-20) \qquad \frac{-44}{-4} \qquad 21 \div (-7) \qquad -\left(\frac{-3}{-2}\right)$$

4. Which of the quotients are equivalent to 5? Select all that apply.

 $\frac{5}{-1}$

$\square$ $\frac{-15}{-3}$

$\square$ $\frac{-5}{-1}$

$\square$ $\frac{-15}{3}$

$\square$ $\frac{-5}{1}$

5. Which of the quotients are equivalent to $-\left(\frac{48}{17}\right)$? Select all that apply.

$\square$ $\frac{-17}{-48}$

$\square$ $\frac{48}{17}$

$\square$ $\frac{48}{-17}$

$\square$ $\frac{-48}{17}$

$\square$ $-2\frac{14}{17}$

6. An elevator steadily descends 500 feet in 20 seconds. How would you express the change in the elevator's height per second?

7. Write three expressions that are equivalent to $\frac{70}{-5}$.

8. **Use Structure** Terry descends 110 feet in 10 minutes inside a cave. Which of the expressions shows Terry's change in position from where he was before descending.

Ⓐ $\dfrac{-110 \text{ feet}}{-10 \text{ minutes}}$

Ⓑ $\dfrac{110 \text{ feet}}{10 \text{ minutes}}$

Ⓒ $\dfrac{10 \text{ feet}}{-110 \text{ minutes}}$

Ⓓ $\dfrac{-110 \text{ feet}}{10 \text{ minutes}}$

9. Gina is hiking from the top of a mountain. In 24 minutes, she walks down the mountainside to a location 1,524 feet from the top of the mountain. If she walks at about the same pace, express Gina's average change in altitude per minute.

10. Can you find the sign of the quotient $\dfrac{-152}{-8}$ before performing the division? Explain.

11. **Higher Order Thinking** If the fraction $\dfrac{294}{x}$ is equivalent to -14, find the value of x.

✅ Assessment Practice

12. Aubrey's monthly bank statement shows a total of $51 in fees for ATM withdrawals. That month, Aubrey made 17 ATM withdrawals.

    Write an equation to represent how each ATM withdrawal fee affected Aubrey's bank balance.

13. Which quotients are equivalent to $-\left(\dfrac{84}{-4}\right)$?

☐ 21

☐ −21

☐ $\dfrac{-42}{2}$

☐ $\dfrac{42}{2}$

☐ $-\left(\dfrac{42}{-2}\right)$

Name: _____

1-9 Additional Practice

Leveled Practice In **1–2**, fill in the boxes to find the quotient.

1. Find the quotient of $\frac{5}{6} \div \left(-\frac{13}{7}\right)$.

$$\frac{5}{6} \div \left(-\frac{13}{7}\right) = \frac{5}{6} \cdot \boxed{}$$

$$= -\frac{\boxed{}}{\boxed{}}$$

2. Simplify the complex fraction 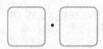.

Rewrite the complex fraction:

$$\boxed{} \div \left(-\frac{2}{5}\right)$$

Write the division as multiplication:

$$\boxed{} \cdot \boxed{}$$

The product is $\boxed{}$.

---

3. Use the division expression $\frac{5}{8} \div \frac{1}{16}$.

   a. Write an equivalent multiplication expression.

   b. **Reasoning** How many times can $\frac{5}{8}$ be divided by $\frac{1}{16}$? How did you decide?

4. Use the division expression $-\frac{10}{13} \div 4\frac{1}{3}$.

   a. Write the multiplication expression equivalent to $-\frac{10}{13} \div 4\frac{1}{3}$.

   b. Find the product.

---

5. Simplify the expression.

   $-3\frac{1}{6} \div \left(-1\frac{4}{9}\right)$

6. Find the quotient.

   $\frac{4}{15} \div -3.4$

7. C.J. says the quotient of $-\frac{3}{4} \div \frac{1}{4}$ is $-\frac{1}{3}$.

   a. What is the correct quotient?

   b. What mistake did C.J. likely make?

     Ⓐ He multiplied the reciprocals of both fractions.

     Ⓑ He added $-\frac{3}{4}$ and $\frac{1}{4}$.

     Ⓒ He multiplied $-\frac{3}{4}$ by $\frac{1}{4}$.

     Ⓓ He multiplied using the reciprocal of $-\frac{3}{4}$.

8. Use the complex fraction $\dfrac{-\frac{8}{11}}{-\frac{3}{5}}$.

   a. Write an equivalent multiplication expression.

   b. Will the quotient of the complex fraction be positive or negative? Explain.

9. Higher Order Thinking Explain why when dividing fractions with the same denominator, you can find the quotient by dividing the numerators. Support your answer with an example using one or more mixed numbers.

☑ Assessment Practice

10. After a heavy rainfall, the water level of a river swelled to the edge of its banks. Any more rain would cause a flood. After a few hours, the river went down $\frac{1}{5}$ inch. Then another storm developed. An additional $\frac{1}{4}$ inch of rainfall was recorded, and the level of the river rose by $\frac{1}{20}$ of the amount of rain that fell during the second storm.

The expression $-\frac{1}{5} + \dfrac{\frac{1}{4}}{\frac{20}{1}}$ represents the change in inches of the water level of the river. Select all the equivalent expressions.

☐ $-\frac{3}{16}$

☐ $\frac{3}{16}$

☐ $-\frac{1}{5} + \frac{1}{4} \cdot \frac{1}{20}$

☐ $-\frac{1}{5} + \frac{1}{4} \div \frac{1}{20}$

☐ $-\frac{1}{5} + \frac{1}{4} + \frac{1}{20}$

Name: _____

1-10 Additional Practice

1. A volleyball team played five games. In those games, the team won by 7 points, lost by 3, lost by 2, won by 4, and won by 9. What was the mean difference in scores over the five games?

2. Use the expression $-8(-2.5 - 7)$.

   a. Simplify the expression by applying the Distributive Property.

   b. Evaluate the expression.

3. The water level of a lake fell by $1\frac{1}{2}$ inches during a $1\frac{2}{3}$-week-long dry spell. Find the average rate at which the water level changed every week.

4. Simplify the expression $2\left(\frac{2}{5}\right) + 2\left(-\frac{1}{5}\right)$.

5. The temperature of a pot of water was 180.3°F and cools at a rate of $-2.5°F$ per minute.

   a. What is the temperature after 20 minutes?

   b. **Look for Relationships** How many minutes will it take to cool from 180.3°F to 100.3°F?

6. **Look for Relationships** An elevator descends at a constant speed. What is the change in elevation after 19 seconds?

Elevator Descent

Time (Sec.)	Change in Elevation (Meters)
1	−2.25
6	−13.5
10	−22.5
12	−27

7. The quiz scores for 6 students who studied together in a math class are in the table.

   a. What is the mean quiz score?

   b. What is the median quiz score?

Quiz Scores

Score	3	4.5	6.5	8	8.5	10

8. Josiah is asked to simplify the expression $\frac{2}{3} + \frac{1}{2}\left(8 + 3\frac{1}{4}\right)$.
   Josiah incorrectly claims that the expression simplifies to $13\frac{1}{8}$.

   a. What is the correct value of the expression?

   b. What error did Josiah likely make?

9. **Higher Order Thinking** The table shows the temperatures of the water in 14 different beakers. What is the average temperature, rounded to the nearest tenth of a degree?

Temperatures in Beakers

Temperature	4.5°C	3.7°C	4.3°C	4.1°C	2.9°C
Frequency	3	4	2	3	2

☑ Assessment Practice

10. A swimming pool is draining at a constant rate. The table shows the proportional relationship between the change in the water level and the number of hours the pool has drained. Complete the table to show the change in water level at 9 and 23 hours.

Draining Swimming Pool

Hours Draining	Change in Water Level (in.)
2	−3.5
9	☐
17	−29.75
23	☐

11. In a classroom there are 6 students who are $5\frac{1}{2}$ feet tall, 2 students who are $4\frac{3}{4}$ feet tall, 4 students who are $4\frac{1}{4}$ feet tall, and 2 students who are 6 feet tall.

    Which expression represents the mean height of the students in the classroom?

    Ⓐ $\dfrac{6\left(5\frac{1}{2}\right) + 2\left(4\frac{3}{4}\right) + 4\left(4\frac{1}{4}\right) + 2(6)}{6 \times 2 \times 4 \times 2}$

    Ⓑ $\dfrac{6\left(5\frac{1}{2}\right) + 2\left(4\frac{3}{4}\right) + 4\left(4\frac{1}{4}\right) + 2(6)}{6 + 2 + 4 + 2}$

    Ⓒ $\dfrac{6\left(4\frac{1}{2}\right) + 2\left(5\frac{3}{4}\right) + 4\left(6\frac{1}{4}\right) + 4(6)}{6 + 2 + 4 + 2}$

    Ⓓ $\dfrac{6\left(4\frac{1}{2}\right) + 2\left(5\frac{1}{2}\right) + 4\left(6\frac{1}{4}\right) + 4(6)}{6 + 2 + 4 + 2}$

Name: _____

Scan for
Multimedia

Leveled Practice In 1–4, write the decimal as a fraction or mixed number.

1. Write $0.\overline{2}$ as a fraction.

Let $x =$ [ ] .

$10x =$ [ ]

$10x - x =$ [ ] − [ ]

$9x =$ [ ]

$x =$ [ ]

So $0.\overline{2}$ is equal to [ ] .

2. Write 1.888... as a mixed number.

Let $x =$ [ ] .

$10x =$ [ ]

$10x - x =$ [ ] − [ ]

$9x =$ [ ]

$x =$ [ ]

So 1.888... is equal to [ ] .

3. Write $0.4\overline{6}$ as a fraction.

Let $x =$ [ ] .

$10x =$ [ ]

$100x =$ [ ]

$100x - 10x =$ [ ] − [ ]

$90x =$ [ ]

$x =$ [ ]

So $0.4\overline{6}$ is equal to [ ] .

4. Write $0.\overline{12}$ as a fraction.

Let $x =$ [ ] .

$100x =$ [ ]

$100x - x =$ [ ] − [ ]

$99x =$ [ ]

$x =$ [ ]

So $0.\overline{12}$ is equal to [ ] .

5. Look for Relationships Brianna asked 45 students if they would vote for her to be student council president. She used her calculator to compare the number of students who said yes with the total number of students. Her calculator showed the result as 0.6222....

a. Write this number as a fraction.

b. How many students said they would vote for Brianna?

6. Write $3.0\overline{1}$ as a mixed number.

7. Write $0.\overline{7}$ as a fraction.

8. **Higher Order Thinking** A reporter determines a baseball player's batting average, which is a ratio of number of hits to number of times at bats. The result is shown on a calculator as 0.2121....

   a. Write this repeating decimal as a fraction.

   b. How many hits would the player be expected to get in 200 at bats? Explain.

9. Write $0.\overline{32}$ as a fraction.

10. Write $2.\overline{5}$ as a mixed number.

☑ Assessment Practice

11. Choose the repeating decimal that is equal to the fraction on the left.

	$0.\overline{24}$	$0.\overline{36}$	$0.2\overline{4}$	$0.3\overline{6}$
$\frac{33}{90}$	☐	☐	☐	☐
$\frac{24}{99}$	☐	☐	☐	☐
$\frac{36}{99}$	☐	☐	☐	☐
$\frac{22}{90}$	☐	☐	☐	☐

12. What fraction is equivalent to $0.\overline{6}$?

2-2 Additional Practice

Scan for Multimedia

1. Is 8.141141114... a rational or irrational number? Explain.

2. Is $\sqrt{72}$ rational or irrational? Explain.

3. Which numbers are rational?

$\sqrt{81}$, $\sqrt{50}$, -12, 0, $\frac{12}{5}$, $6.\overline{54}$

4. Which numbers are irrational?

11, $\sqrt{15}$, -14, $\frac{5}{7}$, $\frac{9}{4}$, $0.151155111555...$

5. Richie says that 2.141441444... is a rational number. Elsa disagrees.

   a. Who is correct?

   b. What is the likely cause of the error?

6. Reasoning Write the side length of the square as a square root. Is the side length a rational number? Explain.

$$A = 121 \text{ ft}^2$$

---

7. Keisha writes the following list of numbers.

$-9, \sqrt{8}, 3.0, \frac{2}{5}, 2.4\overline{2}, \pi$

a. Which numbers are rational?

b. Which numbers are irrational?

8. Higher Order Thinking You are given the expressions $\sqrt{60 + n}$ and $\sqrt{2n + 28}$. What is tthe smallest value of n that will make each number rational?

☑ Assessment Practice

9. Which numbers are rational?

I. 3.222222...

II. 0.112123123412345...

III. 1.589

Ⓐ I only

Ⓑ II only

Ⓒ III only

Ⓓ I and III

Ⓔ II and III

Ⓕ None of the above

10. Classify the following numbers as rational or irrational.

$\frac{2}{3}$ 3.1415926535...   0 $\sqrt{1}$ 7.$\overline{4}$ 15 $\sqrt{3}$

Rational	Irrational

Name: _____

Leveled Practice In **1** and **2**, find the rational approximation.

1. Approximate using perfect squares.

☐ $< 78 <$ ☐

☐ $< \sqrt{78} <$ ☐

☐ $< \sqrt{78} <$ ☐

So $\sqrt{78}$ is between ☐ and ☐.

2. Find the rational approximation of $\sqrt{37}$.

a. Approximate using perfect squares.

☐ $< 37 <$ ☐

☐ $< \sqrt{37} <$ ☐

☐ $< \sqrt{37} <$ ☐

b. Model with Math Locate and plot $\sqrt{37}$ on a number line. Find a better approximation using decimals.

$6.0 \times 6.0 =$ ☐

$6.1 \times 6.1 =$ ☐

$\sqrt{37}$ is closer to ☐.

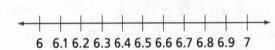

6 6.1 6.2 6.3 6.4 6.5 6.6 6.7 6.8 6.9 7

3. Reasoning Compare $-\sqrt{7}$ and $-3.12345....$ Justify your reasoning.

4. Does $\frac{22}{7}$, -3, $\sqrt{17}$, $\frac{16}{5}$, or -4.5 come first when the numbers are listed from least to greatest? Explain.

5. List the numbers in order from least to greatest.

$\sqrt{5}$, 3.7, $\frac{1}{2}$, -4, $-\frac{9}{4}$

6. Compare 6.51326... and $\sqrt{39}$. Show your work.

7. Ross is comparing $\sqrt{11}$ and $5.\overline{4}$. He says that $\sqrt{11} > 5.\overline{4}$ because $\sqrt{11} = 5.5$.

   a. What is the correct comparison?

   b. **Critique Reasoning** What mistake did Ross likely make?

8. **Higher Order Thinking** If $x = 5$, $y = 6$, and $z = 2$, is $\sqrt{x^2 + y^2 + z^2 + 50}$ rational or irrational? Explain.

☑ Assessment Practice

9. Which list shows the numbers in order from least to greatest?

   Ⓐ $\sqrt{32}$, 5.2, $4\frac{2}{3}$, $\sqrt{17}$

   Ⓑ $\sqrt{17}$, $4\frac{2}{3}$, 5.2, $\sqrt{32}$

   Ⓒ $4\frac{2}{3}$, $\sqrt{32}$, $\sqrt{17}$, 5.2

   Ⓓ 5.2, $\sqrt{17}$, $\sqrt{32}$, $4\frac{2}{3}$

10. The area of a square picture frame is 55 square inches. Find the length of one side of the frame. Explain.

    PART A

    To the nearest whole inch

    PART B

    To the nearest tenth of an inch

Name: _____

2-4 Additional Practice

Leveled Practice In **1** and **2**, evaluate the square root or cube root.

1. Relate the area of the square to the length of each side.

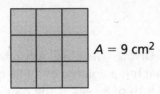

$A = 9$ cm^2

Side length   Side length

☐ cm   ×   ☐ cm

$\sqrt{9} =$ ☐

2. Relate the volume of the cube to the length of each edge.

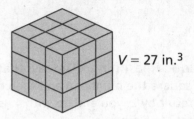

$V = 27$ in.^{3}

Edge length   Edge length   Edge length

☐ in.   ×   ☐ in.   ×   ☐ in.

$\sqrt[3]{27} =$ ☐

3. Ms. Lu is adding a new room to her house. The room will be a cube with volume 4,913 cubic feet. What is the length of the new room?

4. The volume of a box for earrings is 216 cubic centimeters. What is the length of one edge of the box?

5. The area of a square garage is 121 square feet. Will it fit a car that measures 13 feet long? Explain.

6. Nadia wants to enclose a square garden with fencing. It has an area of 141 square feet. To the nearest foot, how much fencing will she need? Explain.

7. Benjamin rents a storage unit that is shaped like a cube. There are 12 identical storage units in each row of the facility. If each storage unit has a volume of 125 cubic feet, what is the length of each row in the facility?

8. Would you classify the number 55 as a perfect square, as a perfect cube, both, or neither? Explain.

9. **Critique Reasoning** Clara says that if you square the number 4 and then divide the result by 2, you end up with 4. Is Clara correct? Explain.

10. **Higher Order Thinking** A fish tank at an aquarium has a volume of 1,568 cubic feet and a depth of 8 feet. If the base of the tank is square, what is the length of each side of the tank?

 **Assessment Practice**

11. Which expression has the least value?
    Ⓐ $\sqrt{81} \cdot 2$
    Ⓑ $\sqrt{81} - \sqrt{25}$
    Ⓒ $\sqrt{64} + \sqrt{25}$
    Ⓓ $\sqrt{64} - 3$

12. On a math test, Ana writes 9 as the solution to $\sqrt[3]{27}$.

    PART A
    Find the correct solution.

    PART B
    What error did Ana likely make on the test?
    Ⓐ Ana cubed 27.
    Ⓑ Ana divided 27 by 3.
    Ⓒ Ana multiplied 27 by 3.
    Ⓓ Ana cubed 3.

2-5 Additional Practice

Scan for Multimedia

Leveled Practice In 1 and 2, solve.

1. $y^2 = 169$

$$\sqrt{\boxed{}} = \pm\sqrt{\boxed{}}$$

$$z = \pm\boxed{}$$

The solutions are $\boxed{}$ and $\boxed{}$.

2. $b^3 = 1{,}000$

$$\sqrt[3]{\boxed{}} = \sqrt[3]{\boxed{}}$$

$$b = \boxed{}$$

3. The volume of a cube shaped crate is 27 cubic feet. What is the length of one edge of the crate?

4. The area of a square patio is 196 square feet. How long is each side of the patio?

5. Solve the equation $c^2 = 4$.

6. Solve the equation $x^2 = 80$.

7. Solve the equation $r^3 = 216$.

8. Solve the equation $v^3 = 36$.

9. Jasmine is a structural engineer. She designs the lift hill of a roller coaster that models the equation $y = x^3$, where y is the height and x is the length from the start of the lift hill. Using this model, how far from the start of the lift hill does the ride reach a height of 343 meters?

10. **Higher Order Thinking** Holly wants to make a frame for a painting. The painting is square and has an area of 225 square inches.

   a. Write an equation to represent the area of the painting, using s for side length. Then, solve the equation for s.

   b. The framing material costs $1.35 per inch. How much will she spend?

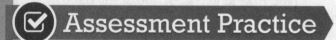

☑ Assessment Practice

11. On a recent homework assignment, Eli needed to solve the equation $g^2 = 49$. He incorrectly wrote $g = 7$.

   PART A

   What is the correct solution?

   PART B

   Critique Reasoning What error did Eli likely make?

   Ⓐ He did not take the square root of 49 correctly since $(-7)^2 \neq 49$.

   Ⓑ He did not solve the equation completely since there is a positive solution as well.

   Ⓒ He did not solve the equation completely since there are two positive solutions.

   Ⓓ He did not solve the equation completely since there are two negative solutions.

12. The zoo is building a new tank for some of its fish. The tank will be a cube able to hold 3,375 cubic feet of water.

   PART A

   Which equation could you use to find the length of each side of the tank?

   Ⓐ $3V = 3,375$

   Ⓑ $\dfrac{3,375}{3} = s$

   Ⓒ $V^3 = 3,375$

   Ⓓ $3,375 = s^3$

   PART B

   How long is each side of the tank?

2-6 Additional Practice

Leveled Practice In **1–4**, use the properties of exponents to write an equivalent expression for each given expression.

1. $5^3 \cdot 5^4 = 5^{3\boxed{}4}$

$= \boxed{}^{\boxed{}}$

2. $\dfrac{4^9}{4^3} = 4^{9\boxed{}3}$

$= \boxed{}^{\boxed{}}$

3. $(7^2)^6 = 7^{2\boxed{}6}$

$= \boxed{}^{\boxed{}}$

4. $2^4 \cdot 6^4 = (\boxed{} \cdot \boxed{})^4$

$= \boxed{}^{\boxed{}}$

5. Simplify the expression $(x^{12})^3$.

6. Simplify the expression $(-12c^5)(3c^4)$.

7. Use the properties of exponents to simplify the expression $\dfrac{5^{22}}{5^{13}}$.

8. Use the properties of exponents to write an equivalent expression for $(3 \cdot 6)^2$.

9. Make Sense and Persevere Compare the two expressions.

    a. Is the expression $a^{12} \cdot a^4$ equivalent to $a^8 \cdot a^8$? Explain.

    b. Does $a^{12} \cdot a^4 = a^8 \cdot a^8$ for all values of a? Explain.

10. A company manufactures photo cells. It uses the expression $(2x^3)^3$ millimeters per second to calculate the maximum capacity of a photo cell with area x^3 square millimeters. Use a property of exponents to simplify this expression.

11. a. Use a property of exponents to write $(2m)^4$ as a product of powers.

    b. **Generalize** Describe the property of exponents that you used.

12. **Higher Order Thinking** Find the two integers, m and n, that make the equation $(2x^n y^2)^m = 4x^6 y^4$ true.

☑ Assessment Practice

13. Select all the expressions equivalent to $(4x^5)(5x^6)$.

    ☐ $(2x^5)(10x^6)$

    ☐ $(4x^5)(6x^5)$

    ☐ $(4x^6)(5x^5)$

    ☐ $20x^{11}$

    ☐ $20x^{30}$

14. You are given the expression $\frac{12^8}{12^4}$ to simplify.

    PART A

    Which equation shows the correct property of exponents to use?

    ⓐ $\frac{a^m}{a^n} = a^{m+n}$

    ⓑ $\frac{a^m}{a^n} = a^{m-n}$

    ⓒ $\frac{a^m}{a^n} = a^{m-a}$

    ⓓ $\frac{a^m}{a^n} = a^{n-m}$

    PART B

    Simplify the expression. Write your answer using exponential notation.

2-7 Additional Practice

Scan for Multimedia

1. Leveled Practice Complete the table to simplify the expression.

Given	Positive Exponent Form	Expanded Form			Simplified Form
5^{-4}	$\dfrac{1}{\boxed{}^{\boxed{}}}$	$\dfrac{1}{\boxed{} \times \boxed{} \times \boxed{} \times \boxed{}}$			$\dfrac{1}{\boxed{}}$

In 2–5, simplify each expression.

2. $135(z^0)$

3. $\dfrac{8}{9^0}$

4. $7^{-2}(-3)^2$

5. $\dfrac{a^{-3}}{b^{-2}}$, for $a = 5$ and $b = 6$.

In 6 and 7, compare the values using >, <, or =.

6. $\left(\dfrac{12}{65}\right)^0 \boxed{} 1$

7. $52^{-4} \boxed{} 1$

In 8 and 9, simplify each expression.

8. $9x^2y^{-3}$, for $x = 5$ and $y = 3$.

9. $14x^{-2}$, for $x = 7$.

10. Julia has to evaluate the expression 4^{-3} before she can join her classmates outside. She decides to use the value of the expression to help choose which activity to do. If the value is greater than 1, she will play basketball. If the value is equal to 1, she will play soccer. If the value is less than 1, she will play tennis. Which activity is Julia going to do today? Explain.

11. You are given the expression -6^{-4}.

    a. Rewrite the expression using a positive exponent.

    b. Reasoning Simplify the expression -6^{-4}. Is the result the same as simplifying the expression $(-6)^{-4}$? Explain.

12. **Higher Order Thinking**

    a. Is the value of the expression $\left(\frac{1}{4^{-2}}\right)^3$ greater than 1, equal to 1 or less than 1?

    b. If the value of the expression is greater than 1, show how you can change one sign to make the value less than 1. If the value is less than 1, show how you can change one sign to make the value greater than 1. If the value is equal to 1, show how you can make one change to make the value not equal to 1.

13. **Construct Arguments** Simplify the expression $18p^0$, assuming that p is nonzero. Will the value of the expression change with different values for p?

✓ Assessment Practice

14. Which expressions are equal to 10^{-5}? Select all that apply.

    ☐ 10^5

    ☐ $10,000$

    ☐ $10,000^{-5}$

    ☐ $\frac{1}{10^5}$

    ☐ $\frac{1}{10,000}$

15. Which expressions have a value less than 1 when $x = 3$? Select all that apply.

    ☐ $\left(\frac{3}{x^2}\right)^0$

    ☐ $\frac{x^0}{3^2}$

    ☐ $\frac{1}{6^{-x}}$

    ☐ $\frac{1}{x^{-3}}$

    ☐ $3x^{-4}$

2-8 Additional Practice

Leveled Practice In **1–3**, use powers of 10 to estimate quantities.

1. Use a single digit times a power of 10 to estimate the number 0.000007328.

   Rounded to the nearest millionth, the number is about ⬚.

   Written as the product of a single digit and a power of ten, this number is ⬚ × 10^⬚.

2. A city has a population of 38,802,500 people. Estimate this population to the nearest ten million.

   Rounded to the nearest ten million, the population is about ⬚.

   Written as the product of a single digit and a power of ten, this number is ⬚ × 10^⬚.

3. The mass of Planet X is 8.46×10^{22} kilograms. The mass of Planet Y is 5,028,000,000,000,000,000,000 kilograms. How many times greater is the mass of Planet X than the mass of Planet Y?

   The mass of Planet Y is about ⬚ × ⬚^⬚ kilograms.

   The mass of Planet X is about ⬚ × ⬚^⬚ kilograms.

   The mass of Planet X is about ⬚ times greater than that of Planet Y.

4. According to a survey, the residents of Country A have approximately 179,300,000 dogs and cats as pets. The same survey reports there are about 5.01×10^7 dogs and cats as pets in Country B. About how many times greater is the number of dogs and cats in Country A than Country B?

5. Estimate 0.00792398 to the nearest thousandth. Express your answer as a single digit times a power of ten.

6. Which number has the greater value, 7×10^{-9} or 6×10^{-4}?

7. On a certain planet, Continent X has an area of 6.23×10^6 square miles and Continent Y has an area of 63,600,000 square miles. How many time larger is Continent Y than Continent X?

8. Dion made $67,785 last year. Express this number as a single digit times a power of ten rounded to the nearest ten thousand.

9. A rectangle has length 8×10^4 millimeters and width 4×10^4 millimeters. How many times greater is the rectangle's length than width?

10. **Construct Arguments** Tara incorrectly estimates 36,591,000,000 meters as 4×10^6 meters. Is she correct? Explain.

11. **Higher Order Thinking** An astronomical unit (AU) is equal to the average distance from the Sun to Earth.

    a. An astronomical unit is about 92,955,807 miles. Use a single digit times a power of ten to estimate this value to the nearest ten million miles.

    b. Venus is about 7.2×10^{-1} AU from the Sun. Mars is about 1.5 AU from the Sun. Which planet is closest to Earth?

Assessment Practice

12. The oldest rocks on Earth are about 4×10^9 years old. For which of these ages could this be an approximation?

    Ⓐ 0.000000004 years

    Ⓑ 3.45×10^9 years

    Ⓒ 3.349999999×10^9 years

    Ⓓ 4,149,000,000 years

13. Express 0.000000648 as a single digit times a power of ten rounded to the nearest ten millionth.

Name: _____

2-9 Additional Practice

  PRACTICE TUTORIAL

Leveled Practice In **1** and **2**, complete the sentences.

1. Express the number 7.901×10^{12} in standard form.

   a. To change this number to standard form, move the decimal point ☐ places to the ☐ .

   b. 7.901×10^{12} is written as ☐ in standard form.

2. You want to express 437,000 in scientific notation. What is the first step?

   a. To change this number to scientific notation, move the decimal point ☐ places to the ☐ .

   b. 437,000 is written as ☐ $\times 10$ ☐ in scientific notation.

---

3. Is 23×10^{-6} written in scientific notation? Justify your response.

4. Is 1.75×10^{6} written in scientific notation? Justify your response.

---

5. Your calculator display shows 5.3E − 9. Express the number in standard form.

---

6. Express the number 621,000 in scientific notation.

7. Express the number 0.00000001073 in scientific notation.

---

8. Express the number 5.2×10^{6} in standard form.

9. Express the number 8.5×10^5 in standard form.

10. Express the number 3.91×10^{-2} in standard form.

11. Express the number 0.00000005864 in scientific notation.

12. Express the number 3.92×10^{-6} in standard form.

13. **Higher Order Thinking** Express the mass 6,200,000 kilograms using scientific notation in kilograms, and then in grams.

✓ Assessment Practice

14. Which of the following numbers are written in scientific notation? Select all that apply.

☐ 34.2×10^9 ☐ 5.99×10^{-9}

☐ 1.80×10^9 ☐ 3.42×10^{-9}

☐ 19.9×10^9 ☐ 18.0×10^{-9}

15. After evaluating an expression, your calculator display shows the result 4.5E−11.

PART A
Express this number in scientific notation.

PART B
Express this number in standard form.

Name: _____

2-10 Additional Practice

Leveled Practice In **1** and **2**, complete the expressions to find the answer.

1. Simplify the expression $(9.6 \times 10^{-8}) \div (2 \times 10^{-15})$. Express your answer in scientific notation.

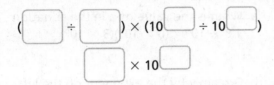

$$\left(\boxed{} \div \boxed{} \right) \times \left(10^{\boxed{}} \div 10^{\boxed{}} \right)$$

$$\boxed{} \times 10^{\boxed{}}$$

2. Simplify the expression $(6.8 \times 10^6) + (3.4 \times 10^6)$. Express your answer in scientific notation.

$$\left(\boxed{} + \boxed{} \right) \times 10^{\boxed{}}$$

$$\boxed{} \times 10^{\boxed{}}$$

$$\boxed{} \times 10^{\boxed{}}$$

3. What is the value of n in the equation $2.6 \times 10^{-2} = (5.2 \times 10^7) \div (2 \times 10^n)$?

4. Simplify $(14.1 \times 10^5) - (2.9 \times 10^5)$. Write your answer in scientific notation.

5. What is the mass of 75,000 oxygen molecules? Express your answer in scientific notation.

Mass of one molecule of oxygen = 5.3×10^{-23} gram

6. **Critique Reasoning** Your friend says that the quotient of 9.2×10^8 and 4×10^{-3} is 2.4×10^5. Is this answer correct? Explain.

7. Find $(3.8 \times 10^7) \times 162$. Write your answer in scientific notation.

8. Find $\frac{10.5 \times 10^{-5}}{2.5 \times 10^{-2}}$. Write your answer in scientific notation.

9. Find $\frac{6.5 \times 10^{11}}{1.3 \times 10^8}$. Write your answer in scientific notation.

10. Find $(7.6 \times 10^3) \times (5.9 \times 10^{12})$. Write your answer in scientific notation.

11. The average U.S. resident uses 100 gallons of water per day. The population of the United States is about 3.23×10^8. About how many gallons of water do U.S. residents use each day? Express your answer in scientific notation.

12. **Higher Order Thinking**

   a. What is the value of n in the equation $1.8 \times 10^n = (6 \times 10^8)(3 \times 10^6)$

   b. Explain why the exponent on the left side of the equation is not equal to the sum of the exponents on the right side.

Assessment Practice

13. Find $(4.54 \times 10^8) - (3.98 \times 10^8)$. When you regroup the decimals, what do you notice about their difference? How does this affect the exponent of the difference?

14. Which expression has the greatest value?

   Ⓐ $(3.23 \times 10^4) + (5.6 \times 10^{-3})$

   Ⓑ $(3.23 \times 10^4) - (5.6 \times 10^{-3})$

   Ⓒ $(3.23 \times 10^4) \times (5.6 \times 10^{-3})$

   Ⓓ $(3.23 \times 10^4) \div (5.6 \times 10^{-3})$

Name: _____

3-1 Additional Practice

Leveled Practice In 1–3, complete the tables of equivalent ratios to solve.

1. There are 3 boys for every 6 girls at a movie. If there are 24 girls, how many boys are at the movie?

Boys	Girls
3	☐
☐	24

There are ☐ boys at the movie.

2. A store sells a package of 25 trading cards for $5.25. What is the cost of one trading card?

Price	Trading Cards
☐	25
☐	1

The unit price is ☐ per card.

3. A car travels 374 meters in 17 seconds. A bus travels 414 meters in 23 seconds. Which vehicle is traveling faster? How much faster?

Car

Meters	Seconds
374	☐
☐	1

Bus

Meters	Seconds
☐	23
☐	1

The ☐ is traveling faster.

It is traveling faster by ☐ – ☐ = ☐ meters per second.

4. In a toy store, the ratio of dolls to teddy bears is 9:3. If the store has 240 dolls, how many teddy bears are in the store?

5. An airplane on autopilot took 5 hours to travel 3,475 kilometers. What was the airplane's speed, in kilometers per hour?

6. Make Sense and Persevere At a supermarket, a 6-ounce bottle of salad dressing costs $1.56. A 14-ounce bottle costs $3.36. A 20-ounce bottle costs $5.60. Which bottle has the lowest cost per ounce?

7. During a thunderstorm, 600 millimeters of rain fell in 30 minutes.

    a. How fast did the rain fall, in millimeters per minute?

    c. **Construct Arguments** Which unit rate do you think is more useful? Explain your reasoning.

    b. How fast did the rain fall, in millimeters per hour?

8. Population density is the number of people per unit of area. The population density of a certain region is 60 people per square kilometer. If the region covers 23 square kilometers, what is the population of the region?

9. **Higher Order Thinking** In basketball, some baskets are worth three points. In one game, the ratio of three-point baskets made to three-point attempts for one team was 3:4. If the team scored 27 points from three-point baskets, how many three-point attempts did the team have?

Assessment Practice

10. Allen is mixing red and yellow paints to make two different shades of orange. To make 1 cup of dark orange paint, he needs 7 ounces of red paint and 1 ounce of yellow paint. To make 2 cups of light orange paint, he needs 13 ounces of yellow paint and 3 ounces of red paint.

    PART A

    Allen buys a 32-oz can of red paint. Does he have enough red paint to make 3 cups of dark orange paint and 3 cups of light orange paint? Explain.

    PART B

    Allen decides to make 3 cups of dark orange paint and 3 cups of light orange paint. How many ounces of yellow paint does he need? Explain.

11. A covered bridge is 8 yards long. In a photograph for sale at a gallery, the bridge is $\frac{5}{12}$ foot long. Which statements are true?

    ☐ One yard of the covered bridge is represented by 1.6 inches in the photograph.

    ☐ One inch on the photograph represents 1.6 yards of the real bridge.

    ☐ A tree that is 3 inches tall in the photograph is 4.8 yards tall.

    ☐ The people walking over the bridge are about 2.5 inches tall in the photograph.

    ☐ A river that is 12 yards wide is 7.5 inches wide in the photograph.

3-2 Additional Practice

Leveled Practice In 1–4, find the unit rate.

1.

Miles	$\frac{1}{5}$	
Hours	$\frac{1}{65}$	

_____ miles per hour

2. $\dfrac{650 \text{ ft}^2}{\frac{2}{3}\text{h}} = \dfrac{650 \div \boxed{}}{\boxed{} \div \boxed{}}$

$= \dfrac{650 \times \boxed{}}{\boxed{} \times \boxed{}} = \dfrac{\boxed{}}{\boxed{}}$

_____ square feet per hour

3. $\dfrac{\frac{1}{7} \text{ inch}}{\frac{1}{14} \text{ minute}}$

_____

4. $\dfrac{\frac{7}{5} \text{ miles}}{\frac{2}{3} \text{ hour}}$

_____

5. A store sells two kinds of candles, scented and unscented. The candles burn at different rates. Which kind of candle burns more in one hour? How much more per hour?

Type of Candle	Rate of Burn
Scented	$\frac{1}{8}$ inch in $\frac{1}{4}$ hour
Unscented	$\frac{1}{9}$ inch in $\frac{1}{3}$ hour

6. In the first $\frac{1}{6}$ hour of a rainstorm, $\frac{1}{10}$ inch of rain fell. If the rain continued to fall at the same rate, how much rain fell in $2\frac{1}{2}$ hours?

7. A recipe calls for $\frac{1}{2}$ cup of Ingredient A for every $1\frac{2}{3}$ cups of Ingredient B. How many cups of Ingredient B do you need when using 4 cups of Ingredient A?

8. Graham drove $42\frac{1}{3}$ miles in $1\frac{1}{3}$ hours.

   a. How many miles did he drive in one hour?

   b. How many hours did he take to drive one mile?

9. **Construct Arguments** Al made a tree house last summer. He started by making a model. The model included a window with a height of $\frac{1}{3}$ inch and a width of $\frac{1}{6}$ inch. The actual window had a height of $\frac{1}{2}$ yard and a width of $\frac{1}{4}$ yard. Was Al's model an accurate representation? Explain.

10. **Be Precise** Yesterday, Noah ran $2\frac{1}{2}$ miles in $\frac{3}{5}$ hour. Emily ran $3\frac{3}{4}$ miles in $\frac{5}{6}$ hour. Anna ran $3\frac{1}{2}$ miles in $\frac{3}{4}$ hour. How fast, in miles per hour, did each person run? Who ran the fastest?

11. **Higher Order Thinking** Josh plans to make birdhouses to sell at a craft fair. The sample of wood he uses has an area of $\frac{1}{5}$ square foot and weighs $\frac{1}{2}$ pound. The local hardware store sells the wood only by the square yard. There are 9 square feet in 1 square yard.

   a. How many pounds of the wood are there in one square yard?

   b. If Josh needs 3 square yards of the wood in all, how many pounds of the wood does he need?

☑ Assessment Practice

12. A map shows the town where Niko lives. The actual distance from Niko's house to his school is 3 miles, and measures one-half inch on the map. The actual distance from Niko's school to the library is 4 miles. How long is this distance on the map?

13. A group of penguins swam $\frac{4}{5}$ mile in $\frac{1}{3}$ hour. Use the table to find how many miles the penguins swam in one hour if they swam at about the same pace for the entire hour.

   The penguins swam [ ] miles in one hour.

Miles		
Hours	$\frac{1}{3}$	

3-3 Additional Practice

Scan for Multimedia

1. At a café, the cook uses a recipe that calls for eggs and milk. The amounts of eggs and milk have a proportional relationship. Complete the table.

Ingredients in Recipe

Number of Eggs	2	3	☐
Cups of Milk	6	☐	12
Milk / Eggs	☐	$\frac{3}{1}$	$\frac{3}{1}$

2. Use Structure Is the relationship between x and y proportional? Explain.

x	y
5	25
6	30
7	35
8	40

3. Construct Arguments Does the table show a proportional relationship between x and y? Explain.

x	y
2	4
4	16
7	79
10	100

4. Does the table show a proportional relationship? If so, what is the value of y when x is $\frac{3}{5}$?

x	y
30	150
$\frac{1}{6}$	$\frac{5}{6}$
199	995
$\frac{2}{15}$	$\frac{2}{3}$

5. In a stationery design, the number of ovals is proportional to the number of squares. How many squares will there be when there are 75 ovals?

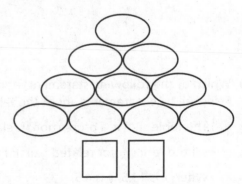

6. The table shows a proportional relationship between x and y.

a. Complete the table.

x	y	$\dfrac{y}{x}$
3	30	
5	50	
7	70	

b. Katerina says the ratio $\dfrac{y}{x}$ is $\dfrac{1}{10}$. What error did she likely make?

7. Higher Order Thinking Do the two tables show the same proportional relationship between x and y? Explain.

x	500	750	1,000
y	1,250	1,875	2,500

x	3	4	5
y	4.2	5.6	7

Assessment Practice

8. During snowstorms, the city sends out trucks to plow. The amount of snowfall and the number of trucks sent out are shown in the table.

Snow Plowing Plan

Snowfall (in.)	Trucks
6	15
8	20
12	30
18	45

PART A

Is the relationship between the amount of snowfall and the number of trucks proportional? Explain.

PART B

For a 23-inch snowfall, how many trucks would the city send out? Explain.

9. Which of the following statements about the table is true? Select all true statements about the table.

x	y
10.5	3.5
15.9	5.3
22.5	7.5
27	9

☐ The table shows a proportional relationship.

☐ All the ratios $\dfrac{y}{x}$ for related pairs of x and y are equivalent to 7.5.

☐ When x is 13.5, y is 4.5.

☐ When y is 12, x is 4.

☐ The unit rate of $\dfrac{y}{x}$ for related pairs of x and y is $\dfrac{1}{3}$.

Name: _____

3-4 Additional Practice

1. A recipe calls for 3 ounces of flour for every 2 ounces of sugar. Find the constant of proportionality.

2. Percy rides his bike 11.2 miles in 1.4 hours at a constant rate. Write an equation to represent the proportional relationship between the number of hours Percy rides, x, and the distance in miles, y, that he travels.

3. Water is dripping from a faucet into a bowl at a constant rate. The number of milliliters of water in the bowl, y, and the time in seconds, x, are shown in the table.

   a. What is the constant of proportionality for the relationship between the number of milliliters of water in the bowl and the time in seconds?

   b. **Model with Math** Write an equation to represent this relationship.

Water from Dripping Faucet

Time in Seconds (x)	Milliliters in Bowl (y)
20	320
35	560
45	720
60	960

4. The relationship between x and y is proportional. When x is 29, y is 275.5.

   a. Find the constant of proportionality of y to x.

   b. Write an equation that relates y and x.

   c. Use the equation to find x when y is 408.5.

5. The width of a row of identical townhouses, y, and the number of townhouses, x, have a proportional relationship. The width of 5 townhouses is 105 ft.

   a. What is the constant of proportionality?

   b. Write an equation that relates the width of a row of townhouses and the number of townhouses.

   c. What would be the width of 9 townhouses in feet?

6. Some friends in college took a road trip to Florida. Use the table to determine whether an equation in the form $y = kx$ can be written for the situation. Explain your answer.

Florida Trip

Hours Driven (x)	Miles Traveled (y)
1.5	82.5
2.5	137.5
4	232
7	350

7. An engineer makes different-size samples of a new material. The table shows volumes and their related masses.

Masses of Samples

Volume in Cubic Centimeters (x)	Mass in Grams (y)
9	90
14	140
25	250

a. What would be the mass of 100 cubic centimeters of the material?

b. What would be the mass of 500 cubic centimeters of the material?

8. Higher Order Thinking The number of pizzas, *y*, and the weight of the shredded cheese topping, *x*, on the pizzas have a proportional relationship. When shredded, a 50-lb block of cheese is enough to make 150 large pizzas.

a. Find the constant of proportionality.

b. How can you use the constant of proportionality to find how much cheese is on one slice of pizza, if there are 8 slices per pizza? Explain.

✓ Assessment Practice

9. For every 3 lemons Chrissy buys at a farm stand, the total cost increases by $1.80.

The constant of proportionality is ☐.

An equation that relates the total cost, *y*, and the number of lemons, *x*, is $y = $ ☐ x.

Use the equation you wrote to complete the table.

Cost of Lemons

Number of Lemons (x)	Total Cost (y)
4	☐
☐	$4.20
☐	$9.00
18	☐

10. For every dozen bagels you buy, the cost increases $15. Which equation represents the cost, *y*, and the number of bagels, *x*?

Ⓐ $y = 1.25 + x$

Ⓑ $y = 15x$

Ⓒ $x = 15y$

Ⓓ $y = 1.25x$

3-5 Additional Practice

Scan for
Multimedia

1. Three friends are buying seashells at the gift shop on the beach. Melanie buys 2 seashells for $0.80. Rosi buys 5 seashells for $2.00. Carlos buys 4 seashells for $1.60.

   Use a graph to determine whether the number of seashells and the cost have a proportional relationship. If so, what is the constant of proportionality and what does it mean?

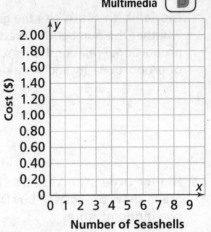

2. For each graph shown, tell whether it shows a proportional relationship. Explain why or why not.

   a.
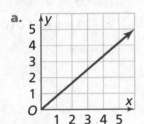

   b.

3. The graph shows the relationship between the distance a taxi travels and the cost of the taxi ride. Is the relationship proportional? Explain.

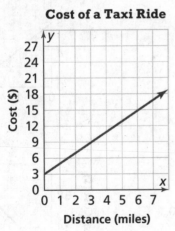

Cost of a Taxi Ride

4. The graph shows a proportional relationship between a family's distance from home and the time spent driving.

Vacation Driving

   a. What does the point (1, 49) represent?

   b. **Look for Relationships** Write an equation that represents the proportional relationship.

5. Two tickets to an ice skating performance costs $36. For five tickets it costs $90, and for nine tickets it costs $162.

    Model with Math Use the graph to determine whether the number of tickets and the cost have a proportional relationship. If so, what is the constant of proportionality and what does it mean?

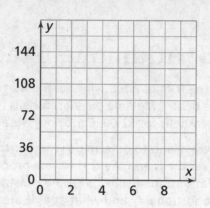

6. **Higher Order Thinking** The table and graph show the costs to buy DVDs at two different stores.

    a. Which store has the better deal on DVDs? Explain.

Store A

Number of DVDs (x)	Cost, $ (y)
2	6.30
3	9.45
4	12.60

Store B

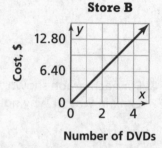

Number of DVDs

    b. How much money will Sheila save if she buys 20 DVDs at the store with the better deal than at the other store?

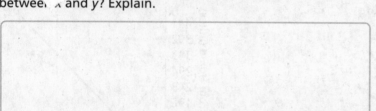

Assessment Practice

7. Does graph at the right show a proportional relationship between x and y? Explain.

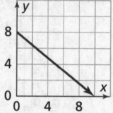

8. The graph at the right shows the relationship between the weight of silver and the total cost. Which of the following statements about the graph are true?

    ☐ The point (0, 0) means that 0 pounds of silver cost $0.00.

    ☐ The point (1, 17) shows the constant of proportionality.

    ☐ The point (4, 68) means that $4.00 is the cost for 68 pounds of silver.

    ☐ The point (2, 34) means that 34 pounds of silver cost $2.00 per pound.

    ☐ The graph shows a proportional relationship.

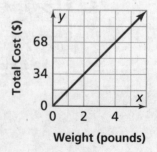

Weight (pounds)

Name: _____

3-6 Additional Practice

In 1 and 2, determine whether you can use proportional reasoning and then solve.

1. The table shows the number of Calories Jane burns while exercising. How many Calories would she burn by exercising for 29 minutes? Explain.

Jane's Exercise

Time in Minutes (x)	Calories Burned (y)
20	220
25	275
30	330
40	440

2. It takes 3 hours for Marty and Cora to weed a garden. How long will it take 6 people to weed the same garden if they all work at the same constant rate? Explain.

3. At a cookout, Mrs. Crawford makes $\frac{8}{9}$ pound of chicken, plus 1 pound for each guest. Is the relationship between the number of guests and pounds of chicken proportional? Explain.

4. How long will it take the jet to travel 5,880 miles?

Passenger Jet Travel

Hours	1	2	3	4
Miles	490	980	1,470	1,960

5. A machine can make 56 parts in 4 hours. It can also make 70 parts in 5 hours. Write an equation that relates the number of parts the machine can make and the time in hours. Predict how many parts the machine can make in 9 hours, 30 minutes.

6. **Look for Relationships** The table shows the relationship between a hedgehog's weight loss and the number of days it has spent in hibernation. How much weight would the hedgehog lose during 115 days in hibernation?

Weight Loss of Hedgehog

Days in Hibernation	Loss in Weight (oz)
8	0.24
28	0.84
75	2.25
93	2.79

7. **Higher Order Thinking** During the first week of the season, Carly averaged 27 points per basketball game. Then she went on a scoring streak. The table shows the increase in the number of points she scored per game from her Week 1 average.

Carly's Scoring

Week	Increase in Points
2	3
3	4.5
4	6

a. If her streak continues into the fifth week, what would Carly's number of points per game be for Week 5?

b. **Be Precise** Describe how the number of points per week changes over the five weeks.

8. **Reasoning** The table shows the numbers of home runs a baseball player hit during spring training and during the regular season for four years. How many home runs would the player likely have hit during the regular season with 3 home runs hit during spring training? Explain.

Home Runs

Spring Training	Regular Season
2	8
4	4
5	20
6	24

✓ Assessment Practice

9. The ratio of pineapple juice to sparkling water that Sylvia and her friends used to make punch last week was 3 : 2. They used 4 quarts of water last week. This week, Sylvia and her friends want to make three times as much punch.

PART A

Is the relationship between the amount of pineapple juice and the amount of sparkling water proportional? Explain.

PART B

How much pineapple juice do Sylvia and her friends need for this week's punch?

Ⓐ 18 quarts

Ⓑ 12 quarts

Ⓒ 6 quarts

Ⓓ 3 quarts

Name: _____

4-1 Additional Practice

Scan for
Multimedia

Leveled Practice In **1–2, fill in the boxes to solve.**

1. A school orchestra has 60 members. 20% of the members are percussionists. How many orchestra members are percussionists?

   20% · 60 players

   The number of percussionists is

   ⬜% of 60

   = ⬜ · 60

   = ⬜ percussionists.

2. Of 800 cars that drove on a street during a week, 0.75% exceeded the 25 miles per hour speed limit by more than 10 miles per hour. How many cars drove over 35 miles per hour?

   The number of cars driving over 35 miles per hour is

   ⬜% of ⬜

   = ⬜ · 800

   = ⬜ drivers

3. An item sells for $40. The sales tax on the item is 8%. What is the sales tax and total cost?

4. When a bush was first planted in a garden, it was 12 inches tall. After two weeks, it was 120% as tall as when it was first planted. How tall was the bush after the two weeks?

5. The number of students in the marching band this year is 125% as many as the number of students in the marching band last year. If there were 36 students in the marching band last year, how many students are in the marching band this year?

6. Joel earns a commission of 5% on the audio equipment he sells, and the store keeps the rest. He sells a $750 amplifier.

   a. How much commission does Joel earn from the sale?

   b. How much does the store keep?

7. Nixon estimates it will take him 5 hours to finish an art project. It actually takes him 320% of the time estimated. How many hours did it take him to finish the project?

8. A contaminant is found in a solution at a level of $\frac{3}{500}$%. What fraction of the solution is this?

9. A bike shop sells you a bicycle for $63 and a helmet for $21. The total cost is 150% of what the shop spent originally.

   a. How much did the shop spend originally?

   b. How much profit did the bike shop earn by selling the bicycle and helmet to you?

10. A newspaper reporter wrote an article about the amount of a toxin found in a river near a factory. In the article, the reporter incorrectly used 0.25 as the decimal form of $\frac{1}{4}$%.

   a. What is the correct way to write $\frac{1}{4}$% as a decimal?

   b. **Reasoning** What was the reporter's likely error?

11. Allie and Sam are ophthalmologists. Allie found that 40% of the 170 patients she saw in a week were near-sighted. Sam found that 25% of the 236 patients he saw in a week were near-sighted.

   a. How many of the patients Allie saw were near-sighted?

   b. How many of the patients Sam saw were near-sighted?

12. **Higher Order Thinking** Kevin's car can go 315 miles on one tank of gas. He used just under 40% of a full tank of gas to get to a sporting event, traveling at an average speed of 60 miles an hour. About how long did it take him to get there? How did you decide?

Assessment Practice

13. A large university accepts 70% of the students who apply. Of the students the university accepts, 25% actually enroll. If 20,000 students apply, how many actually enroll?

   Ⓐ 14,000 students

   Ⓑ 5,000 students

   Ⓒ 3,500 students

   Ⓓ 1,750 students

14. Krystine has a weekend job advertising an upcoming play. She has two options for being paid. Option A is an hourly wage of $7.00. Option B is a 5% commission on tickets sales. She plans to work 8 hours on both Saturday and Sunday. Tickets are sold for $10 each, and Krystine estimates she will sell about 200 tickets. Which option gives Krystine more earnings this weekend?

   Ⓐ Both options give Krystine the same amount of earnings.

   Ⓑ Option A gives Krystine more earnings this weekend.

   Ⓒ Option B gives Krystine more earnings this weekend.

Name: _____

4-2 Additional Practice

Leveled Practice In **1–2**, fill in the boxes to solve.

1. A bike path is 12.5 miles. Dominic is 70% of the way to the end. How far is Dominic on the path?

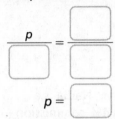

The distance Dominic has biked on the path, p, is ⬚ miles.

2. Of 350 solitaire games that Jay played, he won 154 times. What percent of the games did Jay win?

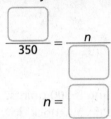

Jay won ⬚ of the solitaire games he played.

3. Construct Arguments A regular tube of toothpaste costs $2.50 for 3.2 ounces. A travel size tube costs $1.00 for 1.2 ounces. Compare the prices and weights using percent to decide which is the better buy.

4. Reasoning Kevin drove his car to a concert. His car can go 400 miles with a full tank of gas. He used 30% of the full tank of gas to get to the concert while traveling 60 miles per hour. How long did it take Kevin to get to the concert?

5. Decide whether the following situation is looking for the percent, the part, or the whole:

The 14 compact cars sold by a dealer on Monday was 56% of the cars sold that day.

6. Investors buy a studio apartment for $240,000. Of this amount, they have a down payment of $60,000.

a. Their down payment is what percent of the purchase price?

b. What percent of the purchase price would a $12,000 down payment be?

7. When a volcano erupts, the height of the peak is reduced and the upper portion is removed. The height of a volcano after it erupted was 8,219.5 feet. This was 85% of the original height. What was the original height?

8. Mei has 60 milliliters of a solution that is 35% nitric acid. How many milliliters of nitric acid does the solution contain?

9. A perfect score in bowling is 300 points. You get a perfect score if you knock down 120 pins in 10 frames. What are the decimal value and the percent of the number of pins knocked down in relation to a perfect score?

10. Higher Order Thinking Nadia is a stockbroker. She earns 4% commission when she sells stocks. Last week, she earned $288 in commission.

a. What was the total amount of her sales?

b. If she earns $14,000 in commission during the year, what was the total value of stocks that Nadia sold?

✓ Assessment Practice

11. Sofi stores water for her turtle tank in a container with a maximum capacity of 64 ounces. The container is filled with 4.8 ounces less than its maximum capacity.

PART A

Sofi accidentally spills 5% of the container's maximum capacity on the counter. To what percent of its capacity is the container now filled?

Ⓐ 87.5%

Ⓑ 12.5%

Ⓒ 87.9%

Ⓓ 95%

PART B

Sofi needs to add 16 ounces of water to her turtle tank. What percentage of the remaining water in the container does she need to use? Explain.

Name: _____

4-3 Additional Practice

Leveled Practice In 1–2, fill in the boxes to solve.

1. A school drama club has 40 members. Of those students, 35% of the members are seventh graders. How many drama club members are seventh graders?

part = percent • whole

$n = \boxed{}\% \cdot \boxed{}$

$n = \boxed{}$

There are $\boxed{}$ seventh graders in the drama club.

2. Greta made 36 out of 60 free throws during a basketball season. What percent of free throws did Greta make?

part = percent • whole

$\boxed{} = p \cdot \boxed{}$

$\dfrac{\boxed{}}{\boxed{}} = \dfrac{p \cdot \boxed{}}{\boxed{}}$

$p = \boxed{}$, or $\boxed{}$%

Greta made $\boxed{}$% of her free throws.

3. A sweater normally costs $35. There is a 25% discount. What is the amount of discount and sale price of the sweater?

4. Find the percent.

132 is what percent of 880?

5. Decide whether the following situation is looking for the part, the percent, or the whole.

81 of 270 pages in a book

6. Dan is watching the birds in his backyard. Of the birds he watches, 9 of them, or 45%, are sparrows. How may birds are in his backyard?

7. The local movie theater decides to raise the ticket prices 25%. The original ticket price was $12.

a. Which percent equation can be used to determine the amount by which the ticket price will increase?

Ⓐ $y = 12 \div 25\%$

Ⓑ $y = 25\% \cdot 12$

Ⓒ $y = 25\% \div 12$

Ⓓ $y = 12 + 25\%$

b. How much will the price of tickets increase? What will be the new ticket price?

8. Ms. Morgan is a science teacher. She found that 30% of her 120 students are athletes. Mr. Gregory is a math teacher. He found that 27, or 15%, of his students are athletes.

   a. Of the part, the whole, and the percent, which information is still unknown to Ms. Morgan? Find this unknown value.

   b. Of the part, the whole, and the percent, which information is still unknown to Mr. Gregory? Find this unknown value.

9. On election day, registered voters go to a polling place to cast their vote.

   a. In a town, 273,600 votes were cast in an election. 57% of those who were registered voted. How many registered voters are there in the town?

   b. Reese claims that if 60% of the registered voters cast 273,600 votes, there would be fewer registered voters than above. Is he correct? Why or why not?

10. A student answers 90% of the questions on a math exam correctly. If he answers 27 questions correctly, how many questions are on the exam?

11. **Higher Order Thinking** Kristen is promoting an upcoming play. She has two options for how she will be paid. Option A is an hourly wage of $7.00. Option B is a 5% commission on all money made during the play. She plans to work 2 days for 8 hours each day. How much money will the play need to bring in for both payment options to be equivalent?

☑ Assessment Practice

12. Lyndie is making reduced copies of a photo that measures 25 centimeters in height. She sets the copy machine to an 80% size reduction.

PART A

Write a percent equation that represents the relationship of the height of the first copy to the height of the original photo.

PART B

Lyndie wants to make another copy that will have a height of 17 cm. The copy machine settings increase or decrease in increments of 5%. Which photo should she make her copy from, the original or her first copy? Explain.

Name: _____

4-4 Additional Practice

Leveled Practice In 1–2, fill in the boxes to find the percent increase or decrease.

1. What is the percent increase?

a. Original quantity: 100   New quantity: 106

Amount of increase:

☐ – ☐ = ☐

Percent increase:

☐ ÷ ☐

= ☐

= ☐ % increase

b. Original quantity: 10   New quantity: 16

c. Original quantity: 50   New quantity: 56

2. What is the percent decrease?

a. Original quantity: 100   New quantity: 88

Amount of decrease:

☐ – ☐ = ☐

Percent decrease:

☐ ÷ ☐

= ☐

= ☐ % decrease

b. Original quantity: 20   New quantity: 8

c. Original quantity: 50   New quantity: 38

---

3. If the original quantity is 15 and the new quantity is 19, which is the best estimate for the percent change?

Ⓐ 25% decrease

Ⓑ 5% decrease

Ⓒ 5% increase

Ⓓ 25% increase

4. 360 is increased by 25%. The result is then decreased by 50%. What is the final number?

---

5. Emily and a friend bought two tickets to see a soccer game. Each ticket cost $8.25. The friends paid a total of $24.50, which included a fee per ticket for parking near the stadium.

a. How much did each friend pay for the parking fee?

b. What percent increase represents the change when parking is included in the final cost? Explain.

6. Critique Reasoning Two trials are conducted for an experiment. In Trial A, the measured value is 240, while the actual value is 200. In Trial B, the measured value is 195, while the actual value is 240. An assistant says that Trial B has the greater percent error. Is the assistant correct? Explain.

7. Carolyn is searching online for tickets to a concert. Two weeks ago, the cost was $30. Now the cost is $39.

    a. What is the percent increase?

    b. What would be the percent increase if the ticket agent charges an additional $4.50 fee with the new ticket price?

8. Emily predicted her car payment to be $250 each month. Her actual car payment is $275 each month. Enrique predicted his car payment to be $200 each month. His actual car payment is $225 each month.

    a. By what percent was Emily's prediction off?

    b. By what percent was Enrique's prediction off?

9. The seventh-grade class is raising money to have a class trip at the end of the year. They began the year with $1,500. Now they have $1,650 in the account.

    a. What is the percent of increase for the money the class has raised?

    b. Make Sense and Persevere The class figured out that if the percent increase is 99% from the beginning of the year, the class will have enough money for every student to go on the field trip. How much money will the class need to raise for every student to go.

10. Give examples of a 100% increase, 100% decrease, and 100% error. Explain each.

11. Higher Order Thinking Suppose the original quantity is 175 and the new quantity is 126. Write an expression that represents the percent change. Find the percent change and express it as a rational number.

☑ **Assessment Practice**

12. In the first week of August, there were 1,060 people at an amusement park. In the second week, there was a 20% decrease in attendance. The park had estimated that 1,500 people would attend the 2nd week. What is the approximate percent error of their estimate?

Name: _____

4-5 Additional Practice

Leveled Practice In 1–2, fill in the boxes to solve.

1. A computer store bought a program at a cost of $10 and sold it for $13. Find the percent markup.

markup = percent markup · cost

$\$\boxed{} = p \cdot \$\boxed{}$

selling price − cost = markup

$\$\boxed{} - \$\boxed{} = \$\boxed{}$

$\dfrac{\boxed{}}{10} = \boxed{} = \boxed{}\%$

The percent markup of the computer program is $\boxed{}$ %.

2. A music store bought a CD set at a cost of $20. When the store sold the CD set, the percent markup was 40%. Find the selling price.

markup = percent markup · cost

$\boxed{} = \boxed{}\% \cdot \$\boxed{}$

cost + markup = selling price

$\$\boxed{} + \$\boxed{} = \$\boxed{}$

The selling price of the CD is $\$\boxed{}$.

3. A store advertises a 20% markdown on a dishwasher that normally sells for $952.

a. Find the price on sale.

b. The markdown is the greatest possible without the store losing money. What does this tell you about the store's cost?

4. Kevin has $24 to buy a gift for his cousin. He found a gift for $22. With 5% sales tax added on, will Kevin have enough money to buy the gift? If so, how much will he pay?

5. Oliver saves 10% of his weekly earnings for living expenses. He usually makes $520 each week. This week he made 10% more. Oliver incorrectly claims that he has $520 left for spending money this week.

a. Calculate the amount of spending money Oliver has left for the week.

b. What error did Oliver likely make?

6. Brianna hoped to get 100 pumpkins from her garden this year. Since the weather was favorable, 20% more pumpkins grew than expected. Unfortunately, animals ate 30% of all the pumpkins that grew.

a. How many pumpkins were left?

b. Is the final number of pumpkins more or less than Brianna had hoped?

7. Gary wants to buy a video game with a selling price of $48, on sale for 50% off. The sales tax in his state is 4.5%.

   a. How much will Gary have to pay in all?

   b. If he has exactly $25, can he afford to purchase the game? Explain.

8. A department store buys 300 shirts for a total cost of $7,200 and sells them for $30 each. Find the percent markup.

9. **Make Sense and Persevere** A diamond ring that normally sells for $1,275 is on sale for $1,020. A ruby ring that normally sells for $290 is on sale for $203.

   a. What is the percent markdown for the diamond ring?

   b. What is the percent markdown for the ruby ring?

   c. Compare the percent markdowns for the two rings.

10. **Higher Order Thinking** Victor paid $415 for a new kayak that he will sell in his shop. He wants to price the kayak so that he can offer a 25% markdown but still keep a markup of 15% of the price he paid for it. What should be the price of the kayak before markdown?

☑ Assessment Practice

11. A store advertises a sale that all items are marked down 30% or more. A life jacket is marked down from $68 to a sale price of $44.20. Is the advertisement true? Explain why or why not.

12. Paul bought a concert ticket for $25. He sold the ticket at a 35% markup, but had to pay the venue a 5% resale fee on the selling price. How much money did he make from selling the ticket?

4-6 Additional Practice

Leveled Practice Use the information to fill in the boxes and solve.

1. Liu deposited $3,500 into a savings account. The simple interest rate is 4%.

   a. How much interest will the account earn in 2 years?

   Interest = interest rate · principal · time

   Interest = ☐ · $ ☐ · ☐

   Interest = $ ☐

   The account will earn $ ☐ in 2 years.

   b. How much interest will the account earn in 10 years?

   Interest = interest rate · principal · time

   Interest = ☐ · ☐ · ☐

   Interest = $ ☐

   The account will earn $ ☐ in 10 years.

2. Elsie's aunt borrows $400 with an interest rate of 1.5%. How much interest will she pay after 4 years?

3. **Reasoning** Suppose Houston deposits $600 into a savings account with a simple interest rate of 2.5%. He wants to keep his deposit in the bank long enough to earn at least $120 in interest. For how many years should Houston keep his deposit in the bank, assuming he does not withdraw or add to the account balance? Explain.

4. **Critique Reasoning** Gil borrows $8,000 for college expenses. He will pay a total of $10,280 after 6 years. Gil says the interest rate is at least 5%. Is he correct? Explain.

5. If the principal, interest rate, or time in a simple interest problem is doubled, and the other two quantities remain constant, how does the simple interest amount change? Explain.

6. **Make Sense and Persevere** Give an example of two principal amounts and two periods of time for which the simple interest earned at 2.42% would be equal. Explain your answer.

7. **Higher Order Thinking** Theodore earned $92.40 in interest after 4 years on a principal of $550. Bella earned $216.00 in interest after 4 years on a principal of $1,500. Which bank would you rather use, Theodore's or Bella's? Explain.

✅ Assessment Practice

8. A certificate of deposit with $600 principal earns 2.5% interest for 6 years.
   Select all options that would earn the same amount of interest.

   ☐ $200 at 5% for 8 years

   ☐ $80 at 75% for 18 months

   ☐ $250 at 10% for 2 years

   ☐ $300 at 2% for 2 years

   ☐ $225 at 10% for 4 years

9. Aaron borrowed money to start a new business. The simple interest rate on the loan is 2.5%. He will pay back the loan by making a total of 12 payments of $266.50 each. How much did he borrow?

5-1 Additional Practice

Leveled Practice In **1–2**, fill in the boxes to evaluate each expression.

1. Evaluate $3.6x + 4.5y$ when $x = 3$ and $y = 7$.

$3.6 \cdot (\boxed{}) + 4.5 \cdot (\boxed{})$

$= (\boxed{}) + (\boxed{})$

$= (\boxed{})$

2. Evaluate $5.5r - 8.35s$ when $r = 12$ and $s = 4$.

$5.5 \cdot (\boxed{}) - 8.35 \cdot (\boxed{})$

$= (\boxed{}) - (\boxed{})$

$= (\boxed{})$

3. Write an expression that represents the weight of an object that weighs 12 pounds and increases by 0.5 pound per month, m.

$\boxed{} + \boxed{}\, m$

For **4–7**, evaluate each expression for the given value of the variable(s).

4. $4c - 3$

   $c = -2$

5. $\frac{1}{3}x + 5$

   $x = -6$

6. $0.3k - 4m$

   $k = 20$ and $m = -2$

7. $-50 + \frac{5}{13}p$

   $p = -26$

8. **Model with Math** Which expression can be used to determine the total weight of b baseballs that weigh 5.25 ounces each and s softballs that weigh 6.5 ounces each?

   Ⓐ $5.25b + 6.5s$

   Ⓑ $6.5b + 5.25s$

   Ⓒ $5.25b - 6.5s$

   Ⓓ $11.75(b + s)$

9. Mark loads a crate that weighs 22.5 pounds and 12 boxes that each weigh 11.25 pounds onto a truck. What is the total weight of the crate and the boxes?

Ⓐ 135 pounds

Ⓑ 157.5 pounds

Ⓒ 270 pounds

Ⓓ 281.25 pounds

10. Model with Math Water evaporates at a rate of 1.5 ounces per day from a container that holds 34 ounces when full. Which expression represents the amount of water remaining in the container after d days?

Ⓐ $1.5 + 34d$

Ⓑ $34 + 1.5d$

Ⓒ $34 - 1.5d$

Ⓓ $32.5d$

11. A freight train traveling at a rate of 22.5 miles per hour is 60 miles from its destination. How far from the destination will the train be in 2.5 hours?

12. An elevator began at an elevation of 85.5 feet and ascended at a rate of 2.75 feet per second. What was the elevation of the elevator after 8 seconds?

13. Higher Order Thinking A full tank that holds 11.6 gallons of gasoline is using 1.45 gallons per hour. Is the tank more than half full of gasoline after 3.5 hours? Explain your answer.

✅ **Assessment Practice**

14. Amanda bought g gallons of paint for $16.55 per gallon and t pints of paint thinner for $5.97 per pint. The store also charges a 10% sales tax.

PART A

Write an expression to represent the total amount that Amanda spent before tax.

PART B

Amanda has $150 to spend. If she buys 8 gallons of paint, does she has enough money left to buy 2 pints of paint thinner? Explain.

Name: _____

5-2 Additional Practice

Scan for
Multimedia

Leveled Practice In 1–3, write an equivalent expression.

1. $8(y - 7)$

2. $-2x + 7$

3. $\frac{3}{5}x + \frac{2}{5} + \frac{3}{5}x$

---

4. Write an equivalent expression for
$h + 5 + 3 - 2h$.

5. Write an expression that is equivalent
to $\frac{2}{8}b + \left(\frac{3}{8}b + \frac{4}{5}\right)$.

---

6. Write two expressions that are equivalent
to $4n - 5$.

7. Write an expression that is equivalent to
$5\left(\frac{3}{2}r - 8\right)$. State the property that justifies
your answer.

---

8. Andre wrote the expression $15(x - 3)$ to represent
the relationship shown in the table.

Write two other expressions that represent
the relationship shown in the table.

x	Value of Expression
0	−45
3	0
5	30
8	75

9. Write an expression that is equivalent to $2.5x + (-5y) - 2.5$.

10. Use the expression $-\frac{3}{7}g + 10$.

   a. Jake said an equivalent expression is $-10 + \frac{3}{7}g$. What was the likely error made by Jake?

   b. Write a correct equivalent expression.

11. Which shows an expression equivalent to $6x + 8 - 4x$?

   Ⓐ $2x - 8$

   Ⓑ $10x + 8$

   Ⓒ $2x + 8$

   Ⓓ $10x - 8$

12. **Higher Order Thinking** The bakery manager at the grocery store marks down the price of bread by 18%. Shanaya purchases 5 loaves of bread. The expression $5(b - 0.18b)$ represents the price of 5 loaves of bread. Write an equivalent expression and write the property that justifies your answer.

✅ Assessment Practice

13. Select all expressions equivalent to $-\frac{2}{3}x + 2$.

   ☐ $-2 - \frac{2}{3}x$

   ☐ $2 - \frac{2}{3}x$

   ☐ $-1 - \frac{2}{3}x + 1$

   ☐ $-\frac{1}{3}x - 4 + 2$

   ☐ $-\frac{2}{3}x - 3 + 5$

14. Diego is building a boat dock. The length of the dock is $(x + 8)$ feet. The width of the dock is $(x + 3)$ feet. Create 2 equivalent expressions to represent the perimeter of the boat dock.

5-3 Additional Practice

In **1–6**, simplify each expression.

1. $5m + 3m$

2. $\frac{3}{5}y + \left(-\frac{6}{5}y\right)$

3. $3.1n - 1.1n$

4. $-2.6c - 2.8c$

5. $-3x + 12x$

6. $-\frac{4}{22}t - \frac{5}{22}t$

7. Which expression is equivalent to $-2v + (-4) + 8 + (-3v)$?

  Ⓐ $-5v$

  Ⓑ $7v$

  Ⓒ $-6v + 5$

  Ⓓ $-5v + 4$

8. Which expression is equivalent to $\frac{3}{14}x + (-1) + (-4) - \frac{2}{7}x$?

  Ⓐ $5\frac{1}{14}x + 5$

  Ⓑ $-5\frac{1}{14}x - 5$

  Ⓒ $-\frac{1}{14}x - 5$

  Ⓓ $\frac{5}{14}x - 5$

For 9–14, simplify the given expression.

9. $-1.3f + 0.4j - 12 - 1 + 2.9f$

10. $n + 4.5 - 0.3n - 3$

11. $8 - 4y + (-2y) + 5$

12. $2.8 - 4.4n - 2n + 7$

13. $11 + (-3) - \frac{1}{8}j - \frac{3}{8}j + 7$

14. $\frac{2}{11}z - \frac{5}{11}z + 4 - \frac{1}{11}z - 8$

15. **Higher Order Thinking** Explain whether $8t - 3y - 4t$ is equivalent to $7t + (-3t) - 3y$.

✓ Assessment Practice

16. **PART A**

An expression in shown.

$\left(\frac{4}{5}x + 1\right) + \left(\frac{2}{5}x - 1\right)$

Create an equivalent expression without parentheses.

PART B

An expression is shown.

$\left(\frac{4}{5}x + 1\right) - \left(\frac{2}{5}x - 1\right)$

Create an equivalent expression without parentheses.

17. Select all the expressions equivalent to $12x - 3 + 2x + 13$.

☐ $17x + 13$

☐ $14x + 10$

☐ $14x + 16$

☐ $10x + 16$

☐ $2(7x + 5)$

5-4 Additional Practice

Leveled Practice In **1–2**, fill in the boxes to expand each expression.

1. $3(t - 2)$

$= (3)\ \boxed{}\ + (3)\ \boxed{}$

$=\ \boxed{}\ +\ \boxed{}$

2. $0.2(y + 2)$

$=\ \boxed{}\ y +\ \boxed{}\ (2)$

$=\ \boxed{}\ +\ \boxed{}$

For **3–6**, write the expanded form for each expression.

3. $2(y + 5x)$

4. $-\frac{1}{2}(y - x)$

5. $a(8 + 2b - 6)$

6. $-2.5(-3 + 4n + 8)$

7. Use the Distributive Property to expand the expression $y(9 - 0.2x)$.

8. Expand the expression $\frac{1}{2}(3 + 4t - 10)$

9. Which expression is equivalent to $\frac{1}{5}(15 + 10x - 5)$?

Ⓐ $2 + 2x$

Ⓑ $2 - 2x$

Ⓒ $-2 + 2x$

Ⓓ $-2 - 2x$

10. **Higher Order Thinking** A carpenter plans to extend the length of a rectangular desk by 7 feet. Let x represent the desk's original length. The expression $9(x + 7)$ represents the area of the desk's surface, where 9 is the width, in feet, and $(x + 7)$ represents the extended length, in feet, of the desk. The carpenter thinks that the area of the extended portion of the desk is 16 square feet.

Which choice below includes the expanded form of the area expression for the desk's surface and the correct area of the extended portion of the desk's surface?

Ⓐ $10x + 16$ and $10x$ square feet

Ⓑ $9x + 63$ and $9x$ square feet

Ⓒ $9x + 7$ and 7 square feet

Ⓓ $9x + 63$ and 63 square feet

11. Write the expanded form of $h(3k - 12.4)$.

12. Use the Distributive Property to write an expression that is equivalent to $2.5(-10 + 3\frac{3}{4}x - 6.2)$.

☑ Assessment Practice

13. An architect plans to build an extension for a rectangular bedroom. The bedroom is 5 meters wide, and the original length of the bedroom is 8 meters. The length of the bedroom's extension, in meters, is represented by x. The expression $5(x + 8)$ represents the area, in square meters, of the bedroom.

PART A

Create an equivalent expression without parentheses.

PART B

What does each term of your expression represent?

Name: _____

5-5 Additional Practice

Leveled Practice In **1–4**, factor the expression.

1. $21a + 9$.

The GCF of 21 and 9 is 3.

$3 \times \boxed{} = 21a$

$3 \times \boxed{} = 9$

The factored expression is $\boxed{}$.

2. $-18y - 27$.

The GCF of -18 and -27 is -9.

$-9 \times \boxed{} = -18y$

$-9 \times \boxed{} = -27$

The factored expression is $\boxed{}$.

3. $8x + 36$

4. $28y - 32$

5. This model shows the area of a field. Write two expressions that represent the area.

6. Josh is trying to factor the expression $-20a - 8 + 12b$.
He writes $-4(5a + 2 + 3b)$.

a. What error did Josh likely make?

b. Factor the expression correctly.

c. Write an equivalent factored expression.

7. What are possible dimensions of the rectangular area at the right?

Area = $27x - 9$

8. Use the expression $14x + 28y + 21$.

   a. Make Sense and Persevere What is the greatest common factor of the expression?

   b. Factor the expression.

9. Laine correctly factors the expression $15a - 6b + 36$. Give two possible answers Laine could have written.

10. Higher Order Thinking A landscaper is adding a stone path around a rectangular patio. The width of the patio, in feet, is represented by x. The length of the patio is 6 feet more than twice the width, as shown. Write two expressions to represent the perimeter of the patio.

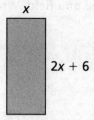

x

$2x + 6$

☑ Assessment Practice

11. Select all the expressions that show a way to factor the expression $-6x + 18$.

   ☐ $-6(x - 3)$

   ☐ $6(-x - 3)$

   ☐ $-6(x + 3)$

   ☐ $6(-x + 3)$

   ☐ $6(x - 3)$

12. An expression is shown.

$-15y - 40$

Create 2 equivalent expressions that show the product of two factors.

5-6 Additional Practice

Scan for
Multimedia

Leveled Practice In 1–4, fill in the boxes to add the expressions.

1. $(3z + 1) + (5 + 7z)$

$= (3z + \boxed{}) + (1 + \boxed{})$

$= \boxed{}z + \boxed{}$

2. $(10x − 4) + (−7 + x)$

$= (10x + \boxed{}) + (−4 + \boxed{})$

$= \boxed{}x + \boxed{}$

3. $(8b + 12) + (3n + 6) + (9b − 4)$

$= (8b + \boxed{}b) + \boxed{}n$

$\quad + (12 + \boxed{} + \boxed{})$

$= \boxed{}b + \boxed{}n + \boxed{}$

4. $\left(\frac{1}{5}x − 4 + 2y\right) + \left(\frac{2}{5}x + 5 − 4y\right)$

$= \left(\frac{1}{5}x + \boxed{}\right) + (−4 + \boxed{})$

$\quad + (2y + \boxed{})$

$= \boxed{}x + \boxed{} + \boxed{}y$

5. Find the sum: $\left(\frac{3}{7}m − 3 + 4n\right) + \left(\frac{2}{7}m − 2n + 6\right)$

6. Find the sum: $(3.2 + 4x) + (18.25 + 6x)$

7. Find the sum: $(6a + 6) + (3x − 2) + (2a + 4)$

8. Combine like terms.

$(−2z − 3) + (4c + 6y) + (7 + 3c)$

9. The width of a rectangle, in feet, is represented by $(3x − 1.5)$. The length of the rectangle, in feet, is represented by $(1.25x + 3)$. Find the perimeter of the rectangle.

10. Elijah opened a checking account with $125 and deposits $25 into it every week. He opened another checking account with $225 and deposits $35 into it every week. Write a simplified expression to represent how much he will have in both accounts after w weeks.

11. Maria has a fence around her triangular garden. The first side is $(y + 4)$ feet long. The second side is 2 feet longer than the first side. The third side is 3 feet less than 2 times the first side. Write a simplified expression to represent the perimeter of the garden.

12. Use the expression $(3t + 4) + (4t + 3)$.

   a. Find the sum.

   b. Explain how you know which terms can be combined to find the sum.

13. **Higher Order Thinking** The expression $3.5d + 5$ represents the number of miles Erin ran last week when she ran 5 miles on Sunday and 3.5 miles each day after Sunday. The expression $2.5d + 3$ represents the number of miles Luis ran last week when he ran 3 miles on Sunday and 2.5 miles each day after Sunday.

   a. Write an expression that can be used to determine the total amount Erin and Luis ran last week.

   b. What is the total number of miles that Erin and Luis ran through Thursday of last week?

✓ Assessment Practice

14. A grocery store conducted a survey to determine its customers' favorite type of fruit.

PART A

Write an expression for each type of fruit if n customers were surveyed.

30 more than two-fifths of the customers chose bananas.	10 fewer than one-fifth of the customers chose apples.	5 more than one-fifth of the customers chose oranges.

PART B

Write a simplified expression to represent all the customers who chose either bananas or oranges.

5-7 Additional Practice

Scan for
Multimedia

Leveled Practice In **1–2**, fill in the missing signs or numbers.

1. Write an equivalent expression to
$m - (8 - 3m)$ without parentheses.

$m \bigcirc 8 \bigcirc 3m$

$= m \bigcirc 3m \bigcirc 8$

$= \boxed{} \; m \bigcirc 8$

2. Write an equivalent expression to
$-2(1.5h + 5) - 4(-0.5 + 3h)$.

$-2 \cdot \boxed{} + (-2) \cdot \boxed{} -$

$4 \cdot \boxed{} + (-4) \cdot \boxed{}$

$= \boxed{} \, h + \boxed{} + \boxed{} + \boxed{} \, h$

$= \boxed{} \, h + \boxed{}$

3. A bag of mixed nuts contains almonds and hazelnuts. There are
$(6x + 13)$ nuts in this particular bag, and $(3x - 7)$ of these are hazelnuts.

a. Which expression represents the number of almonds in the bag?

Ⓐ $6x + 13 - (3x - 7)$

Ⓒ $6x + 13 - 3x - 7$

Ⓑ $3x - 7 - 6x + 13$

Ⓓ $3x - 7 - (6x + 13)$

b. There are $\boxed{}$ almonds in the bag.

4. Simplify each expression.

a. $10x - (-7 + 6x)$

b. $12y - (-4 - 8y)$

c. $14z - 3 - (6 - 5z)$

d. $(-9p + 7) - (-9p + 3)$

5. Subtract $(7.8 - 5.1t)$ from $(2.8 - 3.2t)$. Use the Commutative Property to show the difference another way.

6. Critique Reasoning Tim simplified the difference $\frac{1}{2}p - \left(\frac{1}{4}p - 4\right)$ as $\frac{3}{4}p - 4$. Did he find the correct difference? Explain.

In 7–8, subtract the expressions.

7. $(-4b + 15 - 7k) - (6 + 4b - 2k)$

8. $\left(7j + \frac{1}{8}q + 3\right) - \left(\frac{5}{8}q - 11 + 2j\right)$

9. **Higher Order Thinking** Make a conjecture about what happens when expressions are subtracted in the opposite order. What happens when the results are added? Support your conjecture with an example in which several of the signs are negative.

☑ Assessment Practice

10. An expression is shown.

$(0.5n + 0.3) - (0.75n - 0.45)$

Create an equivalent expression without parentheses.

11. Select all pairs of equivalent expressions.

☐ $6x + 13 - (3x - 7)$ and $6x + 13 + (-3x + 7)$

☐ $3x - 7 - 6x + 13$ and $-3(x + 2)$

☐ $6x + 13 - 3x - 7$ and $5x + 10 - 2x - 4$

☐ $3x - 7 - (6x + 13)$ and $-2x - 7 + (5x - 13)$

☐ $-(6x + 13) - (-3x - 7)$ and $-3(x + 2)$

5-8 Additional Practice

Scan for
Multimedia

1. Paul received a coupon for 43% off one item at a clothing store. Let b be the original price of the item. Use the expression $b - 0.43b$ for the new price of the item. Write an equivalent expression by combining like terms.

2. **Use Structure** The area of a rectangular outdoor stage has been extended on one side. The entire new area in square meters can be written as $216 + 12x$. Factor the expression to find the dimensions of the extended stage.

3. A teacher made a copy of a map. To make the map easier to see, the teacher enlarged the area of the map by 38%. Let d represent the area of the original map. The expression $d + 0.38d$ is one way to represent the area of the new map. Write two expressions that represent the area of the new map.

4. The manager of a store increases the price of a popular product by 5%. Let t be the original price of the product. The new price is $t + 0.05t$.

   a. Find an expression equivalent to $t + 0.05t$.

   b. If the original price was $24, what is the new price?

5. A landowner recently sold a large plot of land. The sale decreased his total acreage by 12%. Let v be the original acreage.

   a. Write two equivalent expressions that represent the new acreage.

   b. Use the expressions to describe another way to find the new acreage.

6. Ellena is considering a venue for a party. Let g represent the number of Ellena's guests. Each venue charges a booking fee plus a cost per guest. Ellena wrote the expression $(62 + 35g) - (56 + 27g)$ to represent the difference in cost of one venue over the other.

   Venue 1: $(62 + 35g)$ Venue 2: $(56 + 27g)$

   a. Write an equivalent expression to show the difference in cost.

   b. What information is included from the expression Ellena wrote compared with the equivalent expression?

7. Construct Arguments Cole orders 4 bags of salted potato chips, 3 bags of sour cream and chive potato chips, and 2 bags of barbecue potato chips. Cole finds the cost using the expression $4x + 3x + 2x$, where x is the cost of one bag of chips. Explain a more efficient way to use an expression to work out the cost.

8. Alexander is building a rectangular pen in his backyard for his dog. The pen will have a length of 13 feet and a width of $2x$ feet. Which expression represents the total amount of fencing needed for the pen? Select all that apply.

☐ $2x + 13$

☐ $2x + 26$

☐ $4x + 26$

☐ $4x + 52$

☐ $2(2x + 13)$

9. Higher Order Thinking A customer at a craft store is buying a blank canvas and a set of brushes. The customer has two coupons; one coupon is valid for 35% off all canvases, and the other is valid for 20% off the entire purchase. The customer can only use one coupon. Let c represent the original price of the canvas and b represent the price of the set of brushes.

a. Write two expressions that represent the "35% off all canvases" coupon.

b. Write two expressions that represent the "20% off the entire purchase" coupon.

c. If the original cost of the canvas is $12 and the set of brushes is $16, which option would be the better choice? Explain.

✓ Assessment Practice

10. An art exhibit is made up of four panels that each have the same height.

PART A

Write an expression for the total area in terms of the height, h.

Panel Areas

Panel	Width (ft)
A	5.58
B	6.02
C	4.42
D	3.98

PART B

The panels are placed so that each panel touches the corner of one other panel. No sides overlap. Write an expression for the total perimeter of the panels.

6-1 Additional Practice

1. Look at the paper to the right.

   a. Write an equation to represent the description.

   b. Describe a real-world situation the equation
      could represent.

> **Eight more than four times
> a number is 28.**

2. **Use Structure** Jenna wants to buy a new tablet that costs $242. She
   already has $62 and plans to save $12 per week. If w represents the
   number of weeks until Jenna has enough money to buy the tablet,
   write an equation that can be used to find the value of w.

3. The height of a certain banner is equal to one third of its length. If
   the banner is 5 feet tall, write an equation that can be used to find
   the banner's length, L, in feet.

4. Cameron buys 2.45 pounds of apples and 1.65 pounds of
   pears. Apples and pears each cost c dollars per pound. If the
   total cost after using the coupon shown is $4.12, write an
   equation that can be used to find the value of c.

> **75¢ off
> entire purchase**

5. Mike buys four equally priced DVD's online. Each DVD costs
   the same amount. With a $5.98 shipping charge included, the
   total cost came to $79.94. Write a word equation you could
   use to find the cost of each DVD.

6. A jar contains 18 strawberry-, 24 cherry-, and 19 lime-flavored
   candies. The rest of the candies are chocolate.
   There are 82 candies in all.

   If n represents the number of chocolates in the jar, what equation
   could you use to find n?

7. A rectangle has a length of $3\frac{7}{8}$ inches and an area of $6\frac{15}{16}$ square inches. Write an equation that represents the area of the rectangle in terms of its length and width, w.

Faris wrote this equation to represent a real-world situation.

8. **Reasoning** Write a situation that could go with this equation.

$$6a - 16 = b$$

9. A chef prepares and evenly divides s ounces of beef stock into 3 smaller pans. The chef uses 8 ounces of beef stock from one of the smaller pans, and 34 ounces of beef stock remain in that smaller pan. Write an equation that correctly represents the number of ounces of beef stock, s, that the chef initially prepares.

10. At a wedding reception, an equal number of guests were seated at each of 12 large tables, and 8 members of the wedding party were seated at the main table. The total number of people at the reception, including the bride and groom, was 128. If n represents the number of people seated at each of the large tables, what equation could you use to find the value of n?

11. **Higher Order Thinking** Write a description that represents the equation $7(a + 2) = 91$.

✅ Assessment Practice

12. An orchard contains 132 trees, which are either apple or pear trees. There are 24 apple trees in each of 4 rows.

PART A

If p represents the number of pear trees in the orchard, what equation could you use to find the value of p?

PART B

Write another real-world situation that the equation from Part A could represent.

6-2 Additional Practice

1. Complete the steps to solve the equation $12x - \frac{2}{3} = 83\frac{1}{3}$

$12x - \frac{2}{3} + \frac{2}{3} = \boxed{}$ Addition Property of Equality

$12x = \boxed{}$

$\frac{12x}{12} = \boxed{}$ Division Property of Equality

$x = \boxed{}$

---

2. Use the bar diagram to solve the following equation:
$4d + 5 = 13$

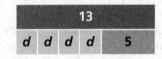

---

3. Solve for p: $0.6p + 4.5 = 22.5$

---

4. Solve the equation $3x + 2 = 17$ using the bar diagram.

---

5. Henry hit 3 more than half as many home runs as Jack hit last season. Henry hit a total of 8 home runs.

   a. Make Sense and Persevere Write an equation you could use to find the number of home runs, x, that Jack hit last season.

   b. Solve your equation to find the number of home runs, x, that Jack hit last season.

---

6. Sarah saved $12.75 every week for a number of weeks, w. She received an additional $25 during the last week in which she saved money. Write and solve an equation to find the number of weeks, w, for which Sarah had saved money if she has $114.25 now.

7. In the year 2000, the number of hazardous waste sites in State X was 8 less than twice the number of hazardous waste sites in State Y. Suppose there were 34 such sites in State X. Write and solve an equation to find the number of hazardous waste sites in State Y, n, in the year 2000.

8. Complete the steps to solve the following equation: $6x + 1.6 = 58$

   a. Apply the Subtraction Property of Equality.

   b. **Use Structure** Apply the Division Property of Equality.

9. a. Write the equation modeled by the bar diagram.

   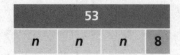

   b. Use the bar diagram to help you solve the equation.

10. **Higher Order Thinking** Each of 5 friends has x action figures in his or her collection. Each friend buys 11 more action figures. Now the 5 friends have a total of 120 action figures.

    a. Write an equation that models the problem.

    b. Solve the equation to find the number of action figures, x, that each friend had originally.

☑ Assessment Practice

11. In one month, Jason earns $32.50 less than twice the amount Kevin earns. Jason earns $212.50. How much does Kevin earn?

12. What steps do you need to take to solve the equation $\frac{1}{2}x + 6 = 18$?

    Ⓐ Add 6. Then multiply by 2.

    Ⓑ Subtract 6. Then divide by 2.

    Ⓒ Add 6. Then divide by 2.

    Ⓓ Subtract 6. Then multiply by 2.

Name: _____

Leveled Practice Use the Distributive Property to solve the equations.

1. $-4(x + 3) = 8$

$$\left(\right) + \left(\right) = 8$$

$$\boxed{} + \boxed{} = 8$$

$$\boxed{} = \boxed{}$$

$$x = \boxed{}$$

$$x = \boxed{}$$

2. $3 = \frac{3}{4}(b - 8)$

$$3 = \left(\right) + \left(\right)$$

$$3 = \boxed{} - \boxed{}$$

$$\boxed{} = \boxed{}$$

$$\boxed{} = b$$

$$\boxed{} = b$$

3. $\frac{1}{6}(p + 24) = 10$

$$\left(\frac{1}{6} \cdot \boxed{}\right) + \left(\frac{1}{6} \cdot \boxed{}\right) = \boxed{}$$

$$p = \boxed{}$$

4. $\frac{3}{5}(a + 5.25) = 7.35$

$$\boxed{}(a) + \boxed{}(5.25) = 7.35$$

$$a = \boxed{}$$

5. Use the following equation: $6(t + 12) = 114$

a. Make Sense and Persevere If you apply the Distributive Property to solve the equation, what operation will you need to use first?

b. What operation will you use last?

6. A family buys 5 airline tickets and travel insurance that costs $17 per ticket. The total cost is $1,495. Let x represent the price of one ticket.

a. Write an equation to represent this situation.

b. What is the price of one ticket?

7. Ashley has x dollars. She spends $23.50 on a new top. She decides to keep $\frac{2}{5}$ of what she has left, which is $13.80. How many dollars did Ashley have originally?

8. The equation at the right has been incorrectly solved.

   a. What error was made?

   $$-4(6 - b) = 4$$
   $$-24 - 4b = 4$$
   $$-4b = 28$$
   $$b = -7$$

   b. What is the correct solution?

9. Lasandra wants to center a towel bar on her door that is 29 inches wide. She determines that the distance from each end of the towel bar to the end of the door is 7.75 inches. Write and solve an equation to find the length of the towel bar.

10. **Higher Order Thinking** The ticket price for a concert at a historic music hall includes $6.40 for the concert, $4.80 for the program, and a hall restoration fee. The price for 11 tickets is $128.15.

    a. Write an equation to represent the cost of the hall restoration fee, f.

    b. Solve the equation to find the cost of the hall restoration fee.

☑ Assessment Practice

11. Latrece sells bracelets for a fixed price at the craft show. For every bracelet she sells, she gives her business partner $4. If Latrece sells 18 bracelets for a total of $207, how much money will Latrece keep from each bracelet sold?

12. What series of steps would result in the correct solution to the equation $-8(0.5y - 3) = 3$?

    Ⓐ Distribute -8. Add 24 to both sides. Divide by 4.

    Ⓑ Distribute -8. Subtract 24 from both sides. Divide by 4.

    Ⓒ Distribute -8. Subtract 24 from both sides. Divide by -4.

    Ⓓ Distribute -8. Add 24 to both sides. Divide by -4.

6-4 Additional Practice

1. Solve: $x - 8 \geq -3$
Graph the solutions.

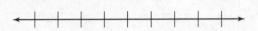

2. Solve: $x + 9 < 12$
Graph the solutions.

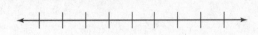

3. Solve each inequality using the Subtraction Property of Inequality.

a. $x + 8 < 20$ **b.** $d + 13 \geq 19$ **c.** $v + 20 > 7$

4. Solve each inequality using the Addition Property of Inequality.

a. $y - 6 \geq 22$ **b.** $g - 13 < 19$ **c.** $p - 20 \leq 7$

5. Chris pays a fee if her bank balance falls below $10 on the statement date. Prior to the statement date, her balance was −$3.46. Then, Chris made a deposit, d, in ample time, so she did not have to pay a fee.

a. Write an inequality to represent this situation.

b. Solve the inequality. Describe the meaning of the solution.

6. Construct Arguments Haley solves the inequality $-13 \geq r + 7$ and graphs the solution on a number line with a solid circle at −20 and an arrow pointing left. Is she correct? Support your answer, and give the correct description if she is incorrect.

7. Beginning from a depth of 35 feet below the surface, a whale swims upward and jumps to a height of nearly 17 feet above the surface.

    a. Model with Math Use an inequality to model the possible change in the number of feet, r, of the whale's elevation.

    b. Solve the inequality. Explain the meaning in terms of the situation.

8. **Higher Order Thinking** Diego's neighbors paid him to take care of their fish when they went on vacation. He spent $13 of his earnings on a book and $9 on some art supplies. Afterward, he had at most $10 left. Write an inequality to represent how much Diego's neighbors paid him. Then solve the inequality.

☑ Assessment Practice

9. Ani bought a bag to hold her dive weights. The bag's manufacturer claims that it can hold 53 pounds without breaking. Ani has placed 29 pounds in the bag. How many more pounds can she place in the bag before it breaks? Write an inequality to represent the situation. Solve the inequality and graph your solution.

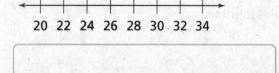

    20 22 24 26 28 30 32 34

10. After pitching $6\frac{2}{3}$ innings in his latest game, Barron has pitched more innings than his $82\frac{1}{3}$ innings pitched last season. How many innings, x, might he have pitched before his latest game? Write an inequality to represent the situation. Solve your inequality.

PRACTICE TUTORIAL

6-5 Additional Practice

Scan for
Multimedia

Leveled Practice For **1–4**, fill in the boxes to solve the inequality.
Then graph the solution.

1. $15x \geq -60$

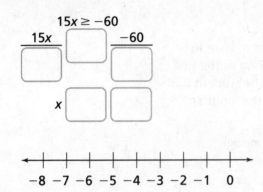

2. $\frac{b}{8} < 8$

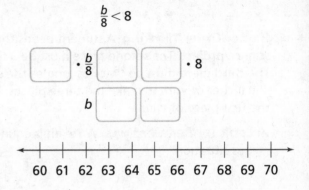

3. $-4n > 36$

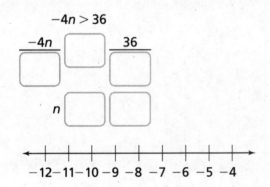

4. $\frac{w}{-10} \leq -20$

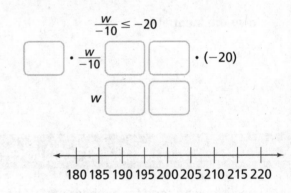

5. Each of 4 family members uses 175 minutes or fewer of their combined
family cell phone plan. At the end of the month, the family does not
have any remaining cell phone minutes. Solve the inequality
$x \div 4 \leq 175$ to find how many cell phone minutes the family
might share each month.

6. Solve each inequality.

    a. $3x < 90$ **b.** $-d \geq 0.5$ **c.** $\frac{v}{32} > -2$

7. A teacher writes the inequality $x \div 6 < -12$ on the board.
Vincent incorrectly solves the inequality and obtains $x < -2$ as the solution.

a. What was Vincent's likely error?

b. What is the correct solution?

8. Higher Order Thinking A student needs three pieces of wire for a science project. The second piece must be 3 times as long as the first. The third piece must be twice as long as the second. The student has 350 inches of wire to make the three pieces. Let x be the length of the first piece of wire.

a. Look for Relationships Write an inequality that models this situation.

b. What are the possible lengths of the shortest piece of wire?

9. Solve the inequality.

$$\frac{g}{-100} \le 6$$

✅ Assessment Practice

10. Luna is buying food for a dinner party. She is going to buy 2 key lime pies that cost $8.99 each. Shrimp costs $8.50 a pound. She needs to spend less than $45 total. Write and solve an inequality to represent the situation. How many pounds of shrimp she can buy? Round to the nearest whole pound.

11. On the first of the month the balance of Amelia's saving account was $60. She plans to deposit $20 each week until she has at least $475 saved. Write and solve an inequality to represent the situation. How many deposits does she need to make to reach her goal?

6-6 Additional Practice

Leveled Practice For **1–4**, solve each inequality.

1. $3 + 4x > 27$

First, subtract [ ] from both sides.

Then [ ] both sides by 4.

$x >$ [ ]

2. $3.5 + 4t \leq 39.5$

3. $12 - 3y < 27$

4. $8 - \frac{1}{4}n \geq 20$

5. a. Solve: $\frac{1}{2}x + 8 \leq 10$

b. Solve: $-3x - 24 \leq -36$

c. Which of the following correctly compares the solutions of the inequalities above?

Ⓐ The inequalities have no common solutions.

Ⓑ The inequalities have only one common solution.

Ⓒ The inequalities have the same solutions.

Ⓓ The inequalities have one uncommon solution.

6. **Make Sense and Persevere** Amelia can spend no more than $89 to rent a car for a day trip. A rental car costs $35 per day plus $0.20 per mile. Write and solve an inequality to find the possible distance in miles, m, that Amelia can drive without exceeding her budget.

7. a. Solve: $9x - 4 > 95$

   b. Solve: $4x + 10 > 54$

   c. Which of the following correctly compares the solutions of the inequalities above?

   Ⓐ The inequalities have the same solutions.

   Ⓑ The inequalities have only one common solution.

   Ⓒ The inequalities have one uncommon solution.

   Ⓓ The inequalities have no common solutions.

8. **Higher Order Thinking** The inequalities $\frac{1}{5}x + 7 \leq 11$ and $-\frac{1}{5}x - 7 \geq -11$ have the same solutions.

   a. What are the solutions for both inequalities?

   b. Without performing any calculations, how can you tell that the inequalities will have the same solutions?

☑ Assessment Practice

9. Eugene wants to ride his bike at least 40 miles today. The first hour was mostly downhill, and he rode 13 miles. He has 3 more hours to ride. Write and solve an inequality to find how many miles per hour Eugene needs to ride to meet his goal.

6-7 Additional Practice

1. Use the inequality $12 \geq 6(12x + 2)$.

a. Apply the Distributive Property to the right side.

$12 \geq \boxed{} + \boxed{}$

b. Solve the inequality.

$x \leq \boxed{}$

2. Use the inequality $24 \geq 58 + 5(x - 3.8)$.

a. Solve the inequality for x.

b. Which graph shows the solution set of the inequality?

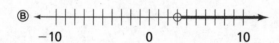

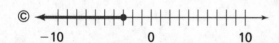

3. Gina shows the steps she took to find the solution of the inequality below.

$19 - 2(1 - x) < 13$

$19 - 2 + 2x < 13$

$2x < -4$

$x > -2$

a. Should Gina have reversed the inequality symbol? Explain.

b. Write the correct solution for the inequality.

4. A rectangle's length, x, is 2 meters greater than its width. If the perimeter of the rectangle is greater than 112 meters, what is the rectangle's possible length, x, in meters?

5. Higher Order Thinking Solve each of the inequalities below for z. Which has -5 as a solution?

$$4(1.1z + 2.75) > -6.6 \qquad\qquad 2(2.1z + 4.5) \leq 21.6$$

6. Use Structure Solve the inequality. Then graph the solutions on the number line.

$$-34 < -2(4x-1)$$

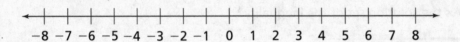

$$-8 \;\; -7 \;\; -6 \;\; -5 \;\; -4 \;\; -3 \;\; -2 \;\; -1 \;\; 0 \;\; 1 \;\; 2 \;\; 3 \;\; 4 \;\; 5 \;\; 6 \;\; 7 \;\; 8$$

✅ Assessment Practice

7. The length of a rectangle is 3 inches longer than its width. The perimeter of the rectangle is less than 30 inches. Write and solve an inequality to find the width of the rectangle.

8. Lani withdrew $20 from her bank account each day for 3 days. Write and solve an inequality to find out how much her starting balance was if she still has more than $212 in her account.

Name: _____

7-1 Additional Practice

Leveled Practice In **1** and **2**, complete the steps to solve for x.

1. $\frac{4}{7}x + \frac{5}{14}x = 39$

$$\frac{\boxed{}}{14}x = 39$$

$$\frac{\boxed{}}{\boxed{}}\left(\frac{\boxed{}}{14}x\right) = \frac{\boxed{}}{\boxed{}}(39)$$

$$x = \boxed{}$$

2. $-12.6x - 4.9x = -154$

$$\boxed{}\ x = -154$$

$$x = \frac{-154}{\boxed{}}$$

$$x = \boxed{}$$

In **3–6**, solve for x.

3. $2.4x - 9.1x + 12.5x = -39.44$

4. $-\frac{5}{6}x - \frac{1}{9}x = -102$

5. $\frac{5}{11}x + \frac{2}{3}x - \frac{1}{6}x = -189$

6. $8.7x - 1.9x = 116.96$

7. Make Sense and Persevere Wayne bought blueberries. He uses $\frac{3}{8}$ of the blueberries to make blueberry bread, $\frac{1}{6}$ of the blueberries to make pancakes, and $\frac{5}{12}$ of the blueberries to make jam. If Wayne uses 69 ounces of the blueberries he bought, how many ounces of blueberries did he buy?

8. Make Sense and Persevere Charlotte buys a ticket to go to a baseball game. The total includes a charge of 7% of the original price for extra fees. If Charlotte pays a total of $44.94, how much was the original price of the ticket?

9. Manuel bought 9 pounds of apples. He has eaten $\frac{3}{4}$ of a pound so far and has $15 worth of apples left. Write and solve an equation to find the cost of the apples per pound to the nearest dollar. How much did the apples cost per pound?

10. **Higher Order Thinking** Solve $\frac{3}{4}h - 12 = 8\frac{5}{8}$.

11. Timothy bought concrete mix for several projects. He used 3.5 bags of concrete mix for a new set of stairs and 2.25 bags of concrete mix for a garden wall. Timothy mixed 345 pounds of concrete in all.

345 pounds	
3.5y	2.25y

   a. **Model with Math** Write an equation that can be represented by the bar diagram.

   b. Solve for y. How many pounds of concrete does each bag make?

12. The community center has a pottery class each month. Each student pays $15 for the class and $27 for materials. This month the pottery class brought in a total of $714. How many students are in the class this month?

☑ Assessment Practice

13. **Construct Arguments** Your friend incorrectly says the solution to the equation $11.2y - 7.4y = 141.36$ is $y = 7.6$. What error did your friend make?

   Ⓐ Divided incorrectly

   Ⓑ Added $7.4y + 11.2y$

   Ⓒ Solved for $\frac{1}{y}$ instead of y

   Ⓓ Subtracted like terms incorrectly

14. Brian scored $\frac{1}{10}$ of the points for his basketball team in the state championship game. Joe scored $\frac{1}{4}$ of the points. Together they scored 21 points. Write an equation to represent the situation. What was the total number of points the team scored?

7-2 Additional Practice

Leveled Practice In **1** and **2**, solve each equation.

1. $6.4n - 10 = 4.4n + 6$

$\boxed{}n - 10 = \boxed{}$

$\boxed{}n = \boxed{}$

$n = \boxed{}$

2. $\frac{1}{3}k + 80 = \frac{1}{2}k + 120$

$\dfrac{\boxed{}}{6}k + 80 = \dfrac{\boxed{}}{6}k + 120$

$\boxed{} = \dfrac{\boxed{}}{6}k + 120$

$\boxed{} = \dfrac{\boxed{}}{6}k$

$\boxed{} = k$

3. You and a friend are doing math homework together. You have to solve the equation $5x + 4x - 68 = 34 - 8x$. Your friend arrives at the answer $x = -2$. Is she correct? Explain.

In **4** and **5**, solve the equation for x.

4. $\frac{5}{8}x + 4 = \frac{3}{8}x + 12$

5. $150 - x - 2x = 120 + 2x$

6. A rental car agency charges $240 per week plus $0.25 per mile to rent a car. The charge for a minivan is $180 per week plus $0.40 per mile. After how many miles is the total charge for each vehicle the same?

7. The Smith family and the Jackson family are having their basements remodeled. The Smith's contractor charges $16.50 per hour plus $289 in supplies. The Jackson's contractor charges $18.75 per hour and $274.60 in supplies. At how many hours of work will the total cost be the same for both families?

8. Jim currently has $1,250 in his bank account and Sally has $1,400 in her bank account. Jim deposits $27.50 per week and Sally deposits $20 per week into her account. After how many weeks will they have the same amount of money?

9. **Higher Order Thinking** The price of Stock A at 9 A.M. was $15.75. Since then, the price has been increasing at the rate of $0.05 per hour. At noon, the price of Stock B was $16.53. It begins to decrease at the rate of $0.13 per hour. If the stocks continue to increase and decrease at the same rates, in how many hours will the prices of the stocks be the same?

 Assessment Practice

10. Solve the equation $\frac{7}{3}x + \frac{1}{3}x = 1 + \frac{5}{3}x$. Show your work.

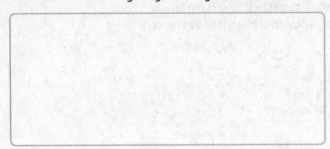

11. Schools A and B are competing in an academic contest. At the beginning of the final round, School A has 174 points and School B has 102 points. In the final round, correct answers earn 10 points and incorrect answers lose 6 points. School A gives the same number of correct and incorrect answers during the final round. School B gives no incorrect answers and the same number of correct answers as School A. The contest ends with the two schools tied.

PART A

Which equation models the scoring in the final round and the outcome of the contest?

Ⓐ $174 + 10x = 102 + 10x - 6x$

Ⓑ $174 + 10x - 6x = 102 + 4x$

Ⓒ $174 - 6x = 102 + 10x$

Ⓓ $174 + 10x - 6x = 102 + 10x$

PART B

How many correct answers does each school give during the final round?

Name: _____

7-3 Additional Practice

Leveled Practice In 1–3, find the value of *x*.

1. Donavon and three friends go to a fair. They each spend $\frac{1}{2}$ of their money on rides. Then they each spend $3 on food. At the end of the day, Donavon and his friends have a total of $8 remaining. How much money did each person bring to the fair?

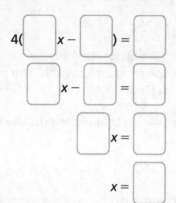

$4(\boxed{}x - \boxed{}) = \boxed{}$

$\boxed{}x - \boxed{} = \boxed{}$

$\boxed{}x = \boxed{}$

$x = \boxed{}$

Donavon and his friends each brought a total of $\boxed{}$.

2. Use the Distributive Property to solve the equation $25 - (3x + 5) = 2(x + 8) + x$.

$25 - \boxed{}x - \boxed{} = 2x + \boxed{} + x$

$20 - \boxed{}x = \boxed{}x + \boxed{}$

$20 - \boxed{}x = \boxed{}$

$\boxed{}x = \boxed{}$

$x = \boxed{}$

3. Use the Distributive Property to solve the equation $2(x - 3) + 3 = 6x - 5$.

$\boxed{}x - \boxed{} + 3 = 6x - \boxed{}$

$\boxed{}x - \boxed{} = 6x - \boxed{}$

$\boxed{}x - \boxed{} = \boxed{}$

$\boxed{}x = \boxed{}$

$x = \boxed{}$

4. Solve the equation $\frac{1}{5}(x - 2) = \frac{1}{10}(x + 6)$.

5. Solve the equation $0.35(x + 4) = 0.25(x - 6)$.

6. If you take $-\frac{3}{10}$ of a number and add 1, you get 10. Let *x* represent the original number.

   a. Write an equation that represents the situation.

   b. What is the original number?

7. Solve the equation $-9(x + 6) = -207$.

8. Use the Distributive Property to solve the equation $5x - 3(x - 3) = -6 + 6x - 5$.

9. Higher Order Thinking The length of a postage stamp is $4\frac{1}{4}$ millimeters longer than its width. The perimeter of the stamp is $124\frac{1}{2}$ millimeters.

a. Write the equation that represents the situation.

b. What is the width of the postage stamp?

c. What is the length of the postage stamp?

Assessment Practice

10. You are given the equation $2(\frac{1}{2}t + 3) = 1$ to solve as part of a homework assignment.

PART A

Describe the first step needed to solve the equation.

PART B

Solve the equation for t. Show your work.

11. Solve the equation $2(6 - x) = 3(x - 1)$.

7-4 Additional Practice

Scan for
Multimedia

1. Leveled Practice Classify the equation $6x + 4x - 1 = 2(5x + 4)$ as having one solution, infinitely many solutions, or no solution.

$$6x + 4x - 1 = 2(5x + 4)$$

$$6x + 4x - 1 = \boxed{} \cdot 5x + \boxed{} \cdot 4$$

$$\boxed{} - 1 = \boxed{} + \boxed{}$$

$$10x - \boxed{} - 1 = 10x - \boxed{} + 8$$

Since $-1 \boxed{} 8$, the equation has $\boxed{}$ solution(s).

For 2–7, classify each equation as having one solution, no solution, or infinitely many solutions. If one solution, write the solution.

2. $48x + 43 = 47x + 43$

3. $2(3x + 8) = 2x + 16 + 4x$

4. $0.4(5x - 15) = 2.5(x + 3)$

5. $3(4x + 2) = 20x - 9x + 2$

6. $4(9x + 6) = 36x - 7$

7. $8(2x + 5) = 16x + 40$

8. Solve $4(2x + 3) = 16x + 3 - 8x + 9$.

9. Solve $8.2(6x - 3) = 7(7x - 1.2)$.

10. **Critique Reasoning** Your friend solved the equation $4x + 24x - 2 = 7(4x + 2)$ and got $x = 16$. What error did your friend make? What is the correct solution?

11. **Higher Order Thinking** Using the expression $x + 3$, write one equation that has one solution, one equation that has no solution, and one equation that has infinitely many solutions. Explain.

    a. one solution

    b. no solution

    c. infinitely many solutions

☑ Assessment Practice

12. Which of the following statements are true about the equation $x + 4x + 4 = 3(2x - 1)$? Select all that apply.

    ☐ Operations that can be used to solve the equation are addition and multiplication.

    ☐ Operations that can be used to solve the equation are addition and division.

    ☐ The equation has infinitely many solutions.

    ☐ The equation has one solution, $x = 7$.

    ☐ The equation has two solutions, $x = 7$ and $x = -7$.

    ☐ The equation has no solution.

13. Two ice cream shops in the mall sell sundaes. Let x equal the number of scoops of ice cream. Larry's Ice Cream Shop's price is represented by the expression $1.2x + 1$. Ice Cream World's price is represented by the expression $0.4(0.3x + 1)$. Which statement is true?

    Ⓐ The two shops charge the same price for a 3-scoop sundae.

    Ⓑ The two shops always charge the same price for sundaes with the same number of scoops.

    Ⓒ The two shops never charge the same price for sundaes with the same number of scoops.

    Ⓓ The two shops charge the same price for a 2-scoop sundae.

PRACTICE   TUTORIAL

7-5 Additional Practice

Scan for
Multimedia

1. Leveled Practice The graph and the table show the total cost of the number of pairs of jeans purchased at two different stores. Which store charges the higher cost for a pair of jeans?

Find the unit rate (constant of proportionality) for Jenny's Jean Store.

$$\frac{\text{cost}}{\text{pairs}} = \frac{\boxed{}}{\boxed{}} = \$\boxed{} \text{ per pair}$$

Find the unit rate (constant of proportionality) for Jean Warehouse.

$$\frac{\text{cost}}{\text{pairs}} = \frac{\boxed{}}{\boxed{}} = \$\boxed{} \text{ per pair}$$

So $\boxed{}$ charges the higher rate.

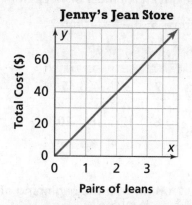

Jenny's Jean Store

Total Cost ($) / Pairs of Jeans

Jean Warehouse				
Pairs of Jeans	2	3	4	5
Total Cost ($)	36	54	72	90

2. The graph shows the average speed of Car 1 which is traveling on a highway. The equation $y = 55x$ represents the average speed of Car 2, where y is the distance in miles and x is the time in hours. Which car is traveling at the greater speed?

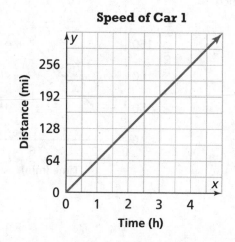

Speed of Car 1

Distance (mi) / Time (h)

3. The graph shows a proportional relationship between the number of workers and weekly cost, in dollars, for a company in its first year. The following year, the company spends $7,200 per 12 employees. Did the rate increase or decrease the following year?

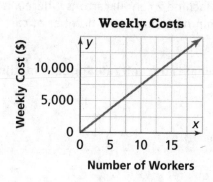

Weekly Costs

Weekly Cost ($) / Number of Workers

4. Corey compares the heights of two plants to see which plant grows more per week. The table shows the relationship between the height and number of weeks for Plant 1. The graph shows the relationship between the height and number of weeks for Plant 2.

Which plant grows at the faster rate?

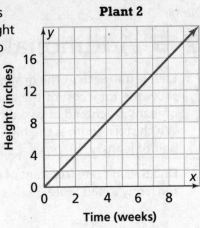

Plant 2

Plant 1				
Weeks	2	3	4	5
Height (inches)	8	12	16	20

5. Higher Order Thinking At the beginning of summer, a maintenance crew refills a swimming pool at a city park. The relationship between the time in hours to fill the pool and the amount of water in the pool is proportional. After 4 hours, the pool holds 5,200 gallons of water.

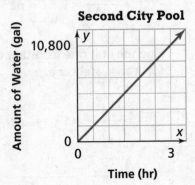

Second City Pool

a. How could you graph this relationship?

b. The same crew refills a second pool as represented by the graph shown. Is the second pool filled at a faster or a slower rate than the first pool? Explain.

✓ Assessment Practice

6. The graph shows the relationship between the time in minutes and the number of milk cartons that Machine 1 can fill. The equation $y = 22x$ describes the rate at which Machine 2 can fill cartons where x is the number of minutes and y is the number of cartons filled.

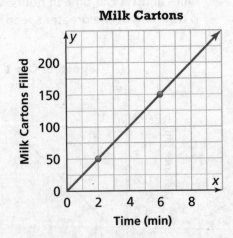

Milk Cartons

PART A

What is the unit rate for each machine?

PART B

Which machine can fill cartons at a faster rate?
How much faster?

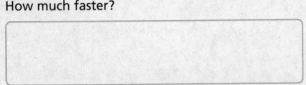

Name: _____

7-6 Additional Practice

Leveled Practice In **1 and 2**, find the slope of each line.

1. Find the slope of the line.

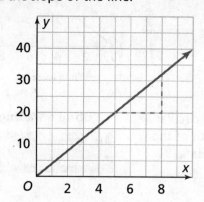

$slope = \dfrac{rise}{run}$

$$= \dfrac{\boxed{}}{\boxed{}} = \boxed{}$$

The slope is $\boxed{}$.

2. Find the slope of the line. Use the two points shown.

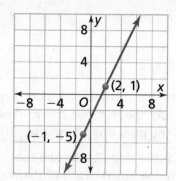

$slope = \dfrac{rise}{run}$

$$= \dfrac{1 - \boxed{}}{\boxed{} - \boxed{}}$$

$$= \dfrac{\boxed{}}{\boxed{}} = \boxed{}$$

The slope is $\boxed{}$.

For **3 and 4**, find the slope of the line that passes through the given points.

3. (0, 10) and (24, 6)

4. (0, 6) and (20, 14)

---

5. The graph shows the number of centimeters a particular plant grows over time.

a. What is the slope of the line?

b. Reasoning What does the slope mean?

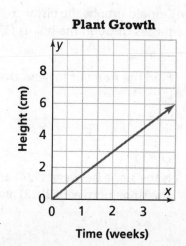

Plant Growth

6. A machinist measures the thickness of a grinding pad every week. The graph shows how many millimeters the grinding pad has worn down.

   a. What is the slope of the line?

   b. Reasoning What does the slope mean?

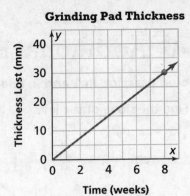

Grinding Pad Thickness

7. **Higher Order Thinking** You use a garden hose to fill a circular wading pool that is 83.6 cm deep. You measure the depth of the water in the pool every 2 minutes. The table shows the data.

   a. What is the slope of the line that represents the change in the depth of the water?

   b. What does this slope mean?

   c. How many minutes will it take to fill the pool?

Filling a Wading Pool

Time (minutes)	Depth of Water (cm)
0	0
2	4.4
4	8.8
6	13.2
8	17.6
10	22.0

8. The graph shows the number of kilometers Gina swims. What is the slope of the line and what does it mean?

Distance Swimming

Assessment Practice

9. Donald graphs the distance he walks over time. The graph passes through the points (3, 12) and (4, 16).

   PART A

   Find the slope of the line that passes through these points.

   PART B

   Is the slope between (1, 4) and (3, 12) the same as the slope between (3, 12) and (4, 16)? Explain.

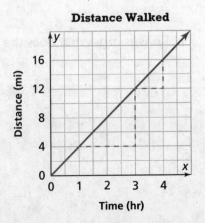

Distance Walked

Name: _____

7-7 Additional Practice

1. **Leveled Practice** The graph shows the number of possible passengers for a given number of roller coaster cars that leave the platform.

   Roller Coaster Passengers

   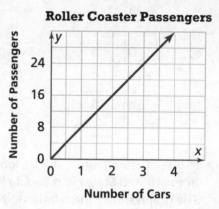

   a. Use two sets of coordinates to write an equation to describe the relationship.

   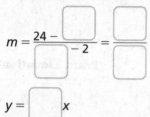

   $$m = \frac{24 - \boxed{}}{\boxed{} - 2} = \frac{\boxed{}}{\boxed{}}$$

   $$y = \boxed{} x$$

   b. Interpret the equation in words.

   Each roller coaster car holds $\boxed{}$ passengers.

2. **Model with Math** The graph relates the actual size of a car in feet to a model of the car in inches. Write an equation that describes the relationship.

   Model Cars

   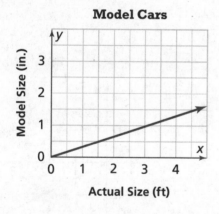

3. Graph the equation $y = \frac{2}{3}x$ on the coordinate plane.

   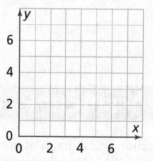

4. A park volunteer plans to work on the park's stone walls for 1 hour every Monday, 1 hour every Wednesday, and 3 hours on Fridays. The graph shows the number of hours he plans to work for a given number of weeks.

   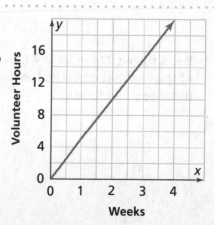

   a. Find the constant of proportionality of the line. Then find the slope of the line.

   b. Write an equation to describe the relationship.

   c. How many hours will the volunteer work in 16 weeks?

5. Model with Math Graph the equation $y = -10x$ on the coordinate plane.

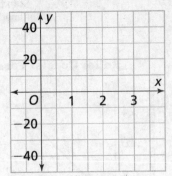

6. Write an equation in the form $y = mx$ for the proportional relationship that passes through the points $(2, -15)$ and $(6, -45)$.

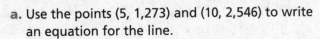

7. Higher Order Thinking The longest aerial tramway in the United States is at Sandia Peak in New Mexico. The graph shows the relationship between the time of the tram ride and its elevation above the base.

a. Use the points $(5, 1,273)$ and $(10, 2,546)$ to write an equation for the line.

b. Interpret the equation in words.

c. Explain why the line is valid only for the first quadrant.

Tram Elevation

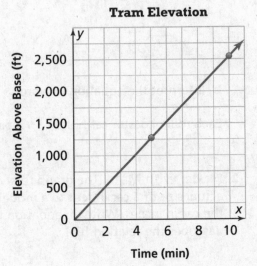

✓ Assessment Practice

8. An equation and a graph of proportional relationships are shown. Which has the greater unit rate?

$$y = \frac{13}{2}x$$

9. Bus X travels 224 miles in 4 hours. Write the equation of the line that describes the relationship between distance y and time x.

Bus X

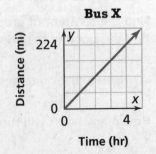

7-8 Additional Practice

Scan for Multimedia

1. Leveled Practice Find the *y*-intercept for the line.

The *y*-intercept is the point where the graph crosses

the ☐ -axis.

The line crosses the *y*-axis at (☐ , ☐).

So, the *y*-intercept is ☐ .

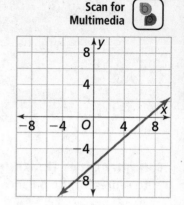

2. The line models the height of a glider *y*, in feet, over *x* hours.

   a. Find the *y*-intercept of the graph.

   b. What does the *y*-intercept represent?

Height of Glider

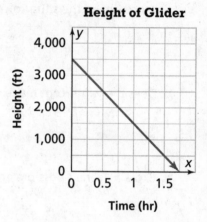

3. Which graph represents a proportional relationship? Explain.

Graph A

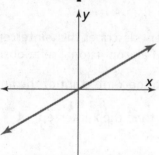

Graph B

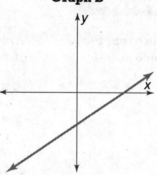

Graph C

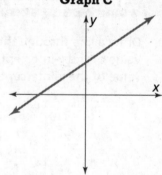

4. The line models the temperature starting at noon on an autumn day.

   a. Find the *y*-intercept of the function.

   b. What does the *y*-intercept represent?

Temperature on Autumn Day

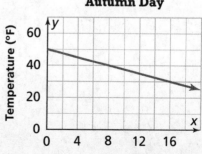

5. Which graph has a *y*-intercept of −5? Explain.

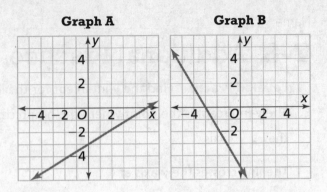

Graph A   Graph B

6. Higher Order Thinking Tasha incorrectly draws this graph to represent the balance in her savings account over time.

a. What is the *y*-intercept of the graph and what does it represent in the situation?

b. Does the *y*-intercept make sense in this situation? Explain.

c. Explain Tasha's possible error.

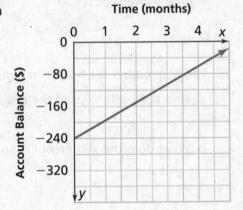

☑ Assessment Practice

7. Draw a line through the point such that the value of the *y*-intercept is the same as the value of the *x*-intercept.

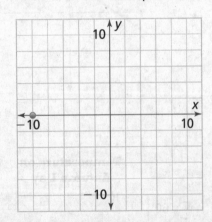

8. Which statement describes the *y*-intercept of the graph of a proportional relationship?

Ⓐ It is equal to the *x*-intercept of the line.

Ⓑ It is greater than the *x*-intercept of the line.

Ⓒ The line intersects the *y*-axis of the graph at the origin.

Ⓓ The line intersects the *y*-axis of the graph above the origin.

Name: _____

7-9 Additional Practice

Scan for
Multimedia

1. Leveled Practice What is the graph of the equation $y = -\frac{1}{4}x + 2$?

The *y*-intercept is ☐, which means the line crosses the *y*-axis

at the point (☐, ☐). Plot this point.

The slope of the line is negative, so it goes ☐ from left to right.

Start at the *y*-intercept. Move down ☐, and then move right

☐. You are now at the point (☐, ☐). Plot this point.

Draw a line to connect the two points.

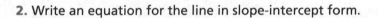

2. Write an equation for the line in slope-intercept form.

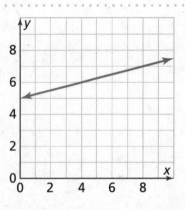

3. Danny is opening a savings account with an initial deposit of $45. He saves $3 per day.

  a. Draw a line to show the relationship between the number of days, *x*, and the total amount in his account, *y*.

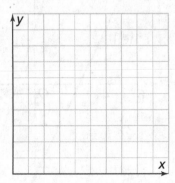

  b. What is the equation of the line in slope-intercept form?

4. Linnea is renting a bike. It costs $4.50 per hour plus a $5 deposit.

  a. Draw a line to show the relationship between the number of hours a bike is rented, *x*, and the total cost of renting a bike, *y*.

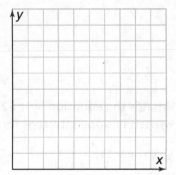

  b. What is the equation of the line in slope-intercept form?

5. The line models a recipe for chicken pie. The recipe calls for 14 ounces of chicken for the first 4 people. The recipe calls for 6 ounces of chicken for each additional person.

a. Write an equation for the line in slope-intercept form, where x is the number of additional people and y is the total number of ounces.

b. If you have 26 ounces of chicken, how many people can you feed?

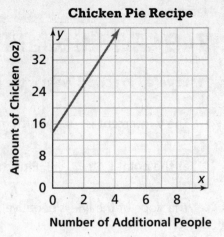

Chicken Pie Recipe

Number of Additional People

6. **Higher Order Thinking** You are given the equation $y - 8 = \frac{3}{5}(x - 5)$ as part of your homework assignment.

a. Write this equation in slope-intercept form.

b. Graph the equation.

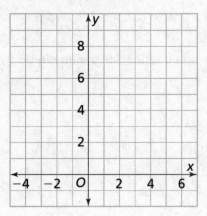

Assessment Practice

7. Write an equation in slope-intercept form for each line at the right.

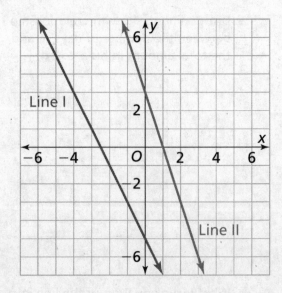

8. What is the equation $5y + 22 = 5x - 33$ written in slope intercept form?

Ⓐ $y = x - 11$

Ⓑ $y = 5x - 55$

Ⓒ $5x = 5y + 55$

Ⓓ $x = y + 11$

Name: _____

8-1 Additional Practice

1. A bagel shop takes a survey to find the approximate percentage of its customers who prefer the new shop hours. What is the population of this survey?

2. During a middle school baseball game, every spectator placed his or her ticket stub into one of several containers. After the game, the coach chose eight people to march in the sportsmanship parade. What is the sample in this situation?

3. Todd and Joan each generate a random sample of the 250 students in Grade 7 at their school. Each sample has 20 students. Todd and Joan each write the numbers 1 through 250 on small pieces of paper and put them in different jars. Then they draw numbers randomly.

Todd's Sample			
19	162	28	33
75	29	180	7
154	125	143	201
14	86	93	66
79	188	55	78

Joan's Sample			
207	13	95	73
28	128	191	48
119	175	212	8
136	39	49	123
20	167	97	147

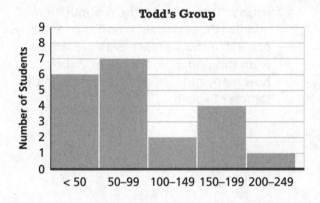

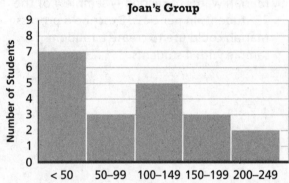

Describe two things you notice about the two random samples taken from the same population.

4. Trevor's science class is studying the rainfall on the first day of each month for one year. Explain why studying the rainfall on the first day of September, October, and November is not a random sample.

5. To predict the performance of her first period class on their next quiz, a teacher randomly selects eight students from the class and takes the mean of their scores on the last quiz. Is this sample representative of the class's performance on the quiz? Explain your reasoning.

6. To predict the outcome of the vote for the school board election, a candidate uses random numbers to pick 100 registered voters. She calls these voters and asks how they plan to vote. Is the sample taken in this problem representative of the population? Explain.

7. Matilda recently took a statistics quiz in her math class. In one question, 45 of 900 visitors at a local craft show were surveyed about the cost of admission to the show. Matilda incorrectly stated that the sample in this situation was represented by the 900 visitors at the craft show.

   a. What is Matilda's error?

   b. What is the actual sample?

8. A movie theater considers upgrading to offer luxury seating. The manager randomly surveys 1,200 residents who live within 10 miles of the theater. What is the sample in this situation?

9. Mariah wants to randomly sample 4 of the 26 students in her class. Describe a process Mariah could use to create a random sample with 4 students.

10. **Higher Order Thinking** A population of middle school students consists of 100 boys and 250 girls. If a representative sample from this population contains 20 boys, how many girls would be expected in this sample? Explain.

Assessment Practice

11. Vanessa's class is studying the number of car commercials on television between 6 P.M. and 8 P.M. for five days. Which is the best sample for Vanessa to use?

   Ⓐ The commercials between 5 P.M. and 7 P.M. on each day

   Ⓑ The first five commercials each of the five days

   Ⓒ The commercials shown between 6 P.M. and 7 P.M. on a randomly chosen day

   Ⓓ The commercials shown between 6:30 P.M. and 7:30 P.M. on three randomly chosen days

PRACTICE TUTORIAL

8-2 Additional Practice

Scan for
Multimedia

**Ages of Students in
Intermediate Swim Class**

1. In an effort to try to convince her mother that she is too old to join the intermediate swim class, Mira, who is 13 years old, gathers data on the ages of a random sample of members of the current intermediate swim class. The results of the data collected by Mira are displayed in the dot plot shown.

   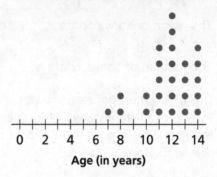

   Age (in years)

   a. The data are clustered between

   ⬚ and ⬚ years old.

   b. Based upon the data collected, is it likely that Mira will be able to convince her mother that she is too old to join the intermediate swim class? Explain.

2. The following dot plots show the amount of time it takes each randomly sampled student to complete two different sets of math homework problems.

   Set 1

   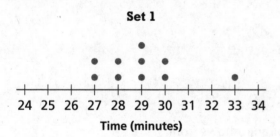

   Time (minutes)

   Set 2

   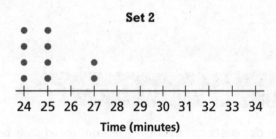

   Time (minutes)

   a. What is the mean time for each set of problems?

   The mean time for Set 1 is ⬚ minutes.

   The mean time for Set 2 is ⬚ minutes.

   b. Reasoning Make a comparative inference based on the mean values.

   Set ⬚ of homework problems is more challenging than Set ⬚.

3. Sonya randomly surveys 26 seventh graders to gather data about the amount of time spent each week using the Internet. Sonya records the data in the dot plot shown. Sonya infers that, on average, most seventh graders use the Internet a little more than 7 hours each week.

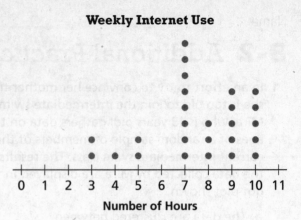

Weekly Internet Use

Number of Hours

a. The mean of Sonya's data is ☐ hours.

b. The median of Sonya's data is ☐ hours.

c. Do the measures of center support Sonya's inference that most seventh graders use the Internet a little more than 7 hours each week? Explain.

4. **Higher Order Thinking** To determine the number of squirrels in a conservation area, a researcher catches, tags, and releases 114 squirrels. He later catches 97 squirrels and finds that 33 of them are tagged. About how many squirrels are in the conservation area? Round to the nearest whole number.

5. **Critique Reasoning** A random survey was conducted about students' favorite vegetables. Ten students voted for green beans, 12 students voted for corn, and 3 students voted for broccoli. Rachel concludes that 240 of the 600 students in the school are expected to prefer green beans. Is her conclusion valid? Explain.

✓ Assessment Practice

6. The dot plots below show the number of calls two radio shows from different radio stations receive each day for a ten-day period. The two shows are on at the same time.

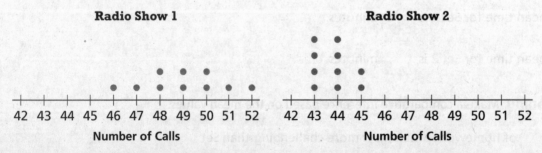

Radio Show 1

Number of Calls

Radio Show 2

Number of Calls

Which of the following inferences based on the median values is valid?

Ⓐ The radio shows receive similar amounts of calls.

Ⓑ Radio Show 1 generally receives more calls.

Ⓒ Radio Show 2 generally receives more calls.

Name: _____

8-3 Additional Practice

1. A student wants to compare the amount of money that two local movie theaters make over a two-week period for the last nightly showing of a particular movie. The following box plots show the data for the amount of money each theater makes over the period. Compare the median of each box plot.

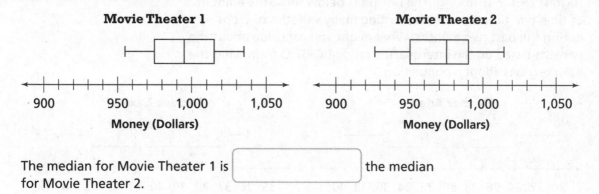

The median for Movie Theater 1 is [   ] the median for Movie Theater 2.

2. The box plots display the speeds, in miles per hour, that two different animals run while hunting. Compare the medians of each dot plot by completing the statement below.

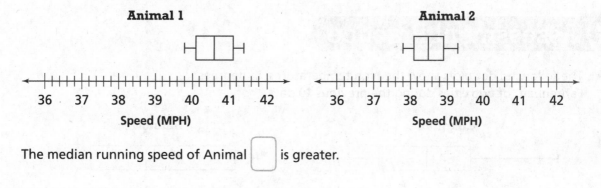

The median running speed of Animal [   ] is greater.

3. The box plots below describe the test scores on a recent math test in two classes. What is the interquartile range (IQR) of the test scores for each class? Make a comparative inference about the populations based on the IQR.

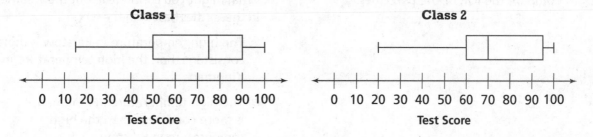

4. Angela is comparing the amount of rainfall over the past month in two cities on days when it rained. In City 1, the range in rainfall is 4.5 centimeters and the IQR is 1.5 centimeters. In City 2, the range is 5 centimeters and the IQR is 3 centimeters. What might you conclude about the cities based on the ranges and interquartile ranges?

5. **Higher Order Thinking** The box plots below show the amount of time two farmers spent harvesting many varieties of crops during the past two months. What might you conclude about the harvests based on the interquartile range (IQR)? Explain what the IQR describes about a population.

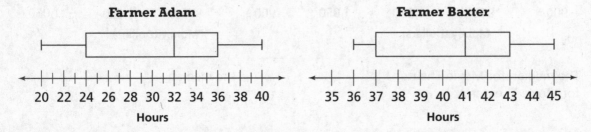

Farmer Adam

20 22 24 26 28 30 32 34 36 38 40
Hours

Farmer Baxter

35 36 37 38 39 40 41 42 43 44 45
Hours

☑ Assessment Practice

6. The following dot plots show the high temperatures, in degrees Fahrenheit, of two cities during the previous 10 days.

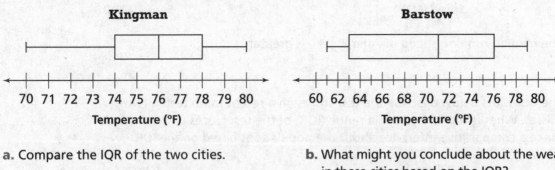

Kingman

70 71 72 73 74 75 76 77 78 79 80
Temperature (°F)

Barstow

60 62 64 66 68 70 72 74 76 78 80
Temperature (°F)

a. Compare the IQR of the two cities.

b. What might you conclude about the weather in these cities based on the IQR?

Ⓐ The high temperature in Barstow is more consistent than the high temperature in Kingman.

Ⓑ The high temperature in Kingman is more consistent than the high temperature in Barstow.

Ⓒ The high temperatures in Kingman and Barstow show similar variability.

Ⓓ The cities of Kingman and Barstow are likely in different states.

Name: _____

8-4 Additional Practice

1. To analyze two schools in the district, the school board randomly surveys 10 students from each school to find how many hours were spent doing homework last night. The data is recorded in the table below.

Number of Hours Spent on Homework										
Xavier Middle School	0	2	2	1	1	4	3	3	4	3
Yates Middle School	1	4	6	3	3	0	2	2	6	3

   a. Which measure of center should the education board use to describe the data? Explain.

   b. What can you infer using the measure of center?

2. The heights of 10 mature plants from each of two different species are recorded in the dot plots below. These samples are representative of each species.

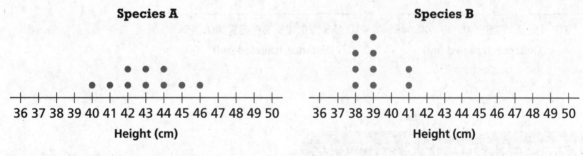

   Species A

   36 37 38 39 40 41 42 43 44 45 46 47 48 49 50
   Height (cm)

   Species B

   36 37 38 39 40 41 42 43 44 45 46 47 48 49 50
   Height (cm)

   a. Find the mean height of each species.

   b. Make an inference about the species based on the mean values.

3. The following dot plots describe the ages of members of two groups of tourists. Suppose the groups of tourists are combined and one tourist, whose age is 46, is randomly selected. Is it *most likely* that this tourist is a member of Group 1 or Group 2? Explain.

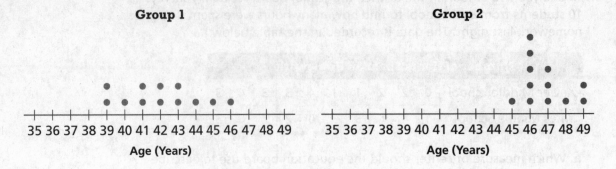

4. **Higher Order Thinking** The dot plots below show the approximate distances players on two soccer teams had to travel to get to the soccer field for their game. Which measure of center should be used to make a comparative inference about the distance traveled by players from each team? Use this measure of center to form a comparative inference.

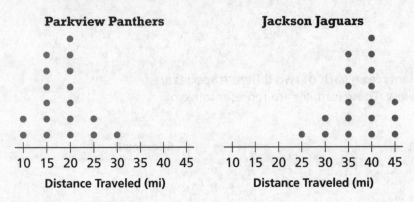

5. Juanita recorded samples of the lengths of the shadows cast by elm trees in two of her neighbors' yards at the same time of day. The median of the sample from Neighbor X's yard is 20 feet. The median of the sample from Neighbor Y's yard is 50 feet. Which is a comparative inference that Juanita can make from the median values?

Ⓐ There are more elm trees in Neighbor Y's yard than in Neighbor X's yard.

Ⓑ Most of the elm trees in Neighbor X's yard are older than the elm trees in Neighbor Y's yard.

Ⓒ There are more elm trees in Neighbor X's yard than in Neighbor Y's yard.

Ⓓ Most of the elm trees in Neighbor Y's yard are older than the elm trees in Neighbor X's yard.

Name: _____

Scan for
Multimedia

1. A random selection will be made from a bag containing different colored disks. Of the 25 disks in the bag, 5 are yellow, so $P(\text{yellow}) = \frac{5}{25}$.

   a. The probability that a yellow disk will be selected is 0 is [   ].

   b. Complete the sentence to describe the likelihood of randomly selecting a yellow disk.

   It is [   ] that a yellow disk will be randomly selected from the bag.

2. Sandra spins the pointer of a spinner. The spinner has four equal sections labeled 1 to 4.

   a. The probability that the pointer will land on a number less than 5 is [   ].

   b. Complete the sentence to describe the likelihood of landing on a number less than 5.

   It is [   ] that the pointer will land on a number less than 5.

3. Michael is planting a garden. The probability that a seed will produce a plant is $\frac{9}{10}$.

   a. The probability that a seed will produce a plant is [   ]%.

   b. Complete the sentence to describe the likelihood that a seed will produce a plant.

   It is [   ] that a seed will produce a plant.

4. A bag contains 80 colored tokens. Of all the tokens in the bag, 25 are black and $\frac{5}{16}$ are red.

   a. Find, in percent form, the probability of choosing a black token and the probability of choosing a red token from this bag.

   b. Compare the likelihood of choosing a black token to that of choosing a red token.

5. Is the spinner shown a fair spinner? Explain why or why not.

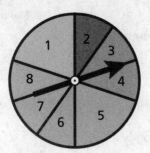

6. Angela is using a number cube for a game with faces labeled 1, 2, 3, 4, 5, and 6. Is the number cube fair? Explain why or why not.

7. Of all 25 marbles in a bag, 3 of the marbles are white.

   a. What is the probability that a white marble will be randomly selected from the bag without looking? Write your answer as a percent.

   b. Describe the likelihood of randomly selecting a white marble from the bag.

8. Higher Order Thinking Greg has a bag that contains 25 colored tiles. Of all the tiles in the bag, 10 are blue. Suppose another bag contains 250 colored tiles. Of all the tiles in this bag, 75 are blue. From which bag is Greg *less* likely to pick a blue tile? Explain.

☑ Assessment Practice

9. Hector made some observations about the numbered cards before his friend turned them face down and rearranged them in a different order without Hector looking. Which of Hector's statements is true if Hector randomly selects one face-down card? Select all that apply.

☐ The probability that Hector will select a card numbered 1 is $\frac{1}{8}$.

☐ The probability Hector will select an odd-number card is greater than 50%.

☐ It is certain Hector will select a card with a label that is greater than 0.

☐ It is impossible for Hector to select a card labeled 2.

☐ It is more likely that Hector will select a card labeled 0 than a card labeled 3.

9-2 Additional Practice

1. Samira is playing a game with the spinner shown.

a. What is the theoretical probability that the pointer will land in a section labeled with the letter A on a given spin? Write as a fraction.

b. Predict how many times the pointer will land in a section labeled with the letter A after 300 spins.

2. The spinner below is divided into eight equal parts. Find the theoretical probability described below as a fraction.

P(greater than 2) = ☐

3. The same number of 7th and 8th graders attend Morgan's school. A student is randomly chosen to raise the flag each day. About how many times is it expected that a 7th grader will raise the flag during the next 30 days of school?

4. Raquel, Richard, Hanne, and Lenny equally split the price of one season ticket so they can take turns attending baseball games. If a season ticket includes 68 games, how many games should Raquel expect to attend this season?

5. A deck of 70 flashcards is numbered 1 through 70. Find the theoretical probability of randomly selecting a card labeled with an even number from the deck of flashcards. Record the answer as a simplified fraction.

P(even number) = ☐

6. A number solid with faces labeled 1 through 16 is rolled. What is the probability that the number 16 will appear facing up when the solid is rolled? Record the answer as a simplified fraction.

P(16) = ☐

7. A 12-sided solid has faces numbered 1 through 12.

a. Find the probability of rolling a number greater than 5.

b. If the 12-sided solid is rolled 180 times, how many times would you expect either a 3, 9, or 11 to be rolled?

8. Camille rolls two number cubes together and records the sum. If she does this 180 times, how many times should she expect the sum to be 7? Explain your answer.

2nd number cube

	1	2	3	4	5	6
1	2	3	4	5	6	7
2	3	4	5	6	7	8
3	4	5	6	7	8	9
4	5	6	7	8	9	10
5	6	7	8	9	10	11
6	7	8	9	10	11	12

1st number cube

9. Based on statistics for the past several seasons, the probability that the best player on a basketball team makes a free throw is $\frac{8}{10}$. The probability that the second-best player makes a free throw is $\frac{13}{20}$. If both players attempt 140 free throws over a season, how many more free throws is the best player expected to make?

10. **Higher Order Thinking** Noah randomly selects one of his eight different pairs of shoes to wear each day. Of his eight pairs of shoes, Noah has two pairs of boots and one pair of loafers. For how many days of the next 264 is it expected that Noah will wear either boots or loafers?

☑ Assessment Practice

11. The spinner at the right is divided into 8 equal sections.

PART A Find the theoretical probability described below. Write your answer as a simplified fraction.

P(number less than 6) =

PART B

About how many times would you expect the pointer to land on a number less than 6 if the pointer is spun 300 times? Explain your answer.

9-3 Additional Practice

1. An eighth-grade class rolls a number cube with faces labeled 1 through 6. The results of 50 rolls are recorded in the table below. Find the relative frequency that a number less than 4 is rolled.

Number Cube Rolls

Outcome	1	2	3	4	5	6
Frequency	6	4	8	12	10	10

A number less than 4 was rolled [   ] times.

The number cube was rolled [   ] times.

The relative frequency of rolling a number less than 4 is [   ] %.

2. Ellen flipped a coin 80 times. The coin landed heads up 44 times and tails up 36 times. Compare the theoretical and experimental probabilities of the coin landing tails up.

Theoretical probability = [   ] %.

Experimental probability = [   ] %.

The theoretical probability is [   ]

than the experimental probability.

3. After many studies, a researcher finds that the probability that a word-recognition program correctly interprets a hand-written word is $\frac{9}{10}$. How many words out of 40 would the researcher expect the program to correctly interpret?

4. The table shows a student's results from spinning the pointer 30 times.

Spinner Frequency

Outcome	1	2	3	4	5
Frequency	9	5	5	7	4

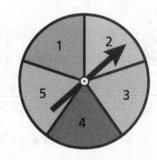

a. Find the theoretical and experimental probabilities that the pointer lands in a section with a number greater than or equal to 2.

Theoretical probability = [   ] %

Experimental probability = [   ] %

b. **Reasoning** What might have caused the theoretical and experimental probabilities to be different?

5. A city council wants to know if residents would like a dog park. They sent a survey to every household in the city. The results of those who responded are shown in the table at the right.

Dog Owners

Number of Dogs in Household	Number of Households
0	513
1	218
2 or more	129

a. What is an appropriate first step in finding the experimental probability that a household has 2 or more dogs?

Ⓐ Find the product of the number of households with one dog and the number with two or more dogs.

Ⓑ Find the difference of the number of households with two or more dogs and the number with no dogs.

Ⓒ Find the sum of the number of households for each category.

Ⓓ Find the difference of the number of households with no dogs and the number with one dog or more.

b. What is the experimental probability that a household has 2 or more dogs?

6. **Higher Order Thinking** The manager of a restaurant wants to add two new side dishes to the menu. She surveys customers about side dish preferences and records the results in the table shown at the right.

Restaurant Menu

Preferred Side Dish	Number of Customers
Baked Potato	127
Steamed Broccoli	44
Asparagus	95
Sweet Potato	104

a. Find the experimental probability that a customer prefers either baked potato or asparagus.

b. Find the experimental probability that a customer prefers either steamed broccoli or sweet potato.

☑ Assessment Practice

7. Hakeem randomly draws equal-sized cards labeled with letters A, B, C, D, and F from a hat and records the results in the table. Compare the theoretical and experimental probabilities of randomly drawing a card that is labeled with the letter C.

Letter	Frequency
A	36
B	50
C	111
D	59
F	44
Total	300

9-4 Additional Practice

PRACTICE   TUTORIAL

1. Four groups must present their final projects to the class. The groups are listed alphabetically from Group A through Group D. The teacher will randomly choose a group to present their project first.

   a. Describe the entire sample space of this event.

   b. List all the outcomes and their probabilities.

2. The spinner shown at the right is used to play a game. Develop a complete probability model for one spin.

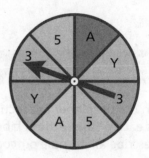

3. A box contains green marbles and blue marbles. Yosef shakes the box and randomly draws a marble. He records the color in the table at the right and places the marble back into the box. Yosef repeats the process 50 times.

   a. Develop a complete probability model for choosing a marble.

   Choosing Marbles

Green	Blue
36	14

   b. Based on the experimental probability, about how many times will Yosef draw a green marble if he draws a total of 75 marbles?

4. The table shows data from a random survey of juice preferences.

   a. List the events from the sample space and their probabilities based on the experimental probability.

Type of Juice	Number of People
Orange	75
Apple	112
Kale	63

   b. Based on the experimental data, how many of 400 juice drinkers would be expected to prefer apple or kale juice? Explain.

5. **Higher Order Thinking** A survey of 600 people was conducted to find their favorite book genre. The survey results are shown in the table at the right.

Genre	Number of People
Adventure	102
Comedy	114
Mystery	84
Romance	132

a. How many people responded with a genre other than one of the genres listed?

b. Develop a complete probability model to describe all possible responses, including 'other' as one response.

Assessment Practice

6. An unfair spinner has sections labeled 1, 2, or 3 that are all twice as large as each of the sections labeled 4, 5, or 6. Develop a probability model to describe all possible outcomes of one spin of the spinner.

7. A bag contains green, orange, and purple tennis balls. Corey shakes the bag, randomly selects a tennis ball, records the color in the table shown, and places the ball back into the bag. Corey repeats this process 40 times.

Tennis Balls

Green	Orange	Purple
15	18	7

PART A

Develop a probability model to describe all possible outcomes of a random selection from the bag.

PART B

Corey repeats his process 10 more times and gets these results: 3 green balls, 2 orange balls and 5 purple balls. Explain a possible reason for this outcome.

Name: _____

9-5 Additional Practice

Scan for
Multimedia

1. Before an upcoming soccer tournament, teams are assigned unique uniforms designed with the colors yellow (Y), green (G), orange (O), and purple (P). Each uniform is mostly one color with a different colored stripe.

   Write an organized list using the format (main color, stripe color) to represent the sample space.

2. A tailor designed two pairs of pants (P1 and P2) and five tops (T1, T2, T3, T4, and T5) to create outfits.

   a. Create a tree diagram to display the sample space of possible outfits that consist of a top and a pair of pants.

   b. How many different outfits can the tailor create?

3. Two friends each choose a slice of pizza with one topping. The available toppings are tomatoes (T), jalapeños (J), onions (O), and eggplant (E). Write an organized list using the format (Friend 1, Friend 2) to represent the sample space of toppings chosen between the two friends.

4. Complete the table to represent the sample space of two-digit numbers using the digits 1, 4, 5, and 9. Use the column label as the tens digit and the row label as the ones digit to complete the table.

Sample Space			
1	4	5	9
1			
4			
5			
9			

5. A museum gift shop sells hats with embroidered logos of the museum. The hats are available in small, medium, and large sizes. They are available in the colors red and green.

Make a tree diagram to represent all possible varieties of hats sold at the museum.

6. Higher Order Thinking Vincent forgot the last two digits of his bicycle lock. He remembers that each digit is 5 or greater. Based on the table below, how many possible pairs of digits are there? Make another table to show all possible combinations if he remembers that the first digit is 6, 8, or 9.

	5	6	7	8	9
5	55	65	75	85	95
6	56	66	76	86	96
7	57	67	77	87	97
8	58	68	78	88	98
9	59	69	79	89	99

☑ Assessment Practice

7. A dive shop rents snorkels out to tourists. They have 10 red snorkels, 12 blue snorkels and 7 yellow snorkels. A group of 12 people come in to rent snorkels. They are each given a random color of snorkel. Which of the following is possible? Select all that apply.

☐ 4 people get a red snorkel, 4 people get a blue snorkel and 4 people get a yellow snorkel.

☐ 10 people get a red snorkel, 1 person gets a blue snorkel and 1 person gets a yellow snorkel.

☐ 8 people get a red snorkel, 2 people get a blue snorkel and no one gets a yellow snorkel.

☐ 5 people get red snorkels, no one gets a blue snorkel and 7 people get yellow snorkels.

☐ 2 people get a red snorkel, 2 people get a blue snorkel and 8 people get a yellow snorkel.

9-6 Additional Practice

Scan for
Multimedia

1. The organized list shows all the possible outcomes when three fair coins are flipped. The possible outcomes of each flip are heads (H) and tails (T).

   What is the probability that exactly 1 fair coin lands heads up when 3 are flipped?

   Sample Space

   HHH, HHT,

   HTH, HTT,

   THH, THT,

   TTH, TTT

2. The table shows the possible outcomes of spinning the pointer of the spinner shown at the right and tossing a fair coin.

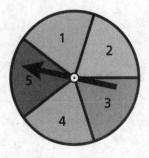

	1	2	3	4	5
H	1, H	2, H	3, H	4, H	5, H
T	1, T	2, T	3, T	4, T	5, T

   $P(1, H) = \boxed{}$

3. A fair coin with sides printed heads and tails is flipped and a golf ball is randomly selected from a bucket that contains 2 yellow and 5 white golf balls.

   a. Develop a complete probability model to describe all the possible outcomes in the sample space.

   b. What is the probability that the coin lands tails up and a white golf ball is selected?

4. The tree diagram below shows all the possible varieties of a T-shirt available in small, medium, and large, and in the colors blue and yellow.

   S < B / Y

   M < B / Y

   L < B / Y

   What is the probability that a medium T-shirt or a yellow T-shirt is randomly selected? Explain.

5. **Higher Order Thinking** A slice of pizza is requested with two randomly selected toppings as listed in the table below at the right. The pizza can have double the amount of a certain topping if the same topping is selected. Complete the *Two-Topping Pizzas* table to represent the sample space of possible topping combinations. Then find the probability that the pizza will have broccoli and olives as the toppings.

Two-Topping Pizzas

	M	P	O	B	S	T
M	M, M	P, M	O, M	B, M	S, M	T, M
P	M, P	P, P				
O	M, O	P, O				
B	M, B					
S	M, S					
T	M, T	P, T	O, T	B, T	S, T	T, T

Pizza Toppings	
Mushrooms (M)	Broccoli (B)
Peppers (P)	Spinach (S)
Olives (O)	Tomatoes (T)

Assessment Practice

6. All possible outcomes of spinning the pointers of two spinners with equal-sized sections labeled 1 through 3 are recorded in the table at the right. Find the probability that the sum of the numbers shown on each spinner will be greater than or equal to 5.

	1	2	3
1	1, 1	1, 2	1, 3
2	2, 1	2, 2	2, 3
3	3, 1	3, 2	3, 3

7. A vowel will be randomly selected from the sample space {a, e, i, o, u}. A number will be randomly selected from the sample space {1, 2}. Draw a tree diagram to represent the possible outcomes of randomly selecting a vowel and a number. Then find the probability of choosing e and 2.

9-7 Additional Practice

Scan for
Multimedia

1. A boy wins a carnival game 50% of the time. He uses a spinner with equal-sized sections labeled 0 through 9 to simulate trials of the game. In the simulation, the numbers 0 through 4 represent winning and the numbers 5 through 9 represent losing. Based on the simulations below that represent the boy playing the game 3 times, what is the probability he wins all 3 times?

   412 750 236 808 904 237 424 648 121 208

2. The probability that a certain bacteria colony thrives in laboratory conditions is 70%. In a simulation conducted using a random-number generator, the numbers 0 through 6 represent bacteria colonies that thrive and the numbers 7 through 9 represent bacteria colonies that do not thrive in the laboratory. There are 4 total bacteria colonies. The results of 6 trials are recorded below. Based on the simulated results, what is the probability that exactly half of the colonies will thrive?

   4285 6903 3829 7871 2868 5137

3. A fair coin is used to simulate the gender of each child in a family with three children. In the simulation, a coin that lands heads up (H) represents a girl, and a coin that lands tails up (T) represents a boy. The simulation is conducted to generate the gender of each child from 10 families. Based on the simulated data recorded below, what is the probability that a family with three children has exactly 2 girls?

Family 1: (H H T)	Family 6: (H H H)
Family 2: (T T T)	Family 7: (T H H)
Family 3: (H H H)	Family 8: (T H T)
Family 4: (H H T)	Family 9: (T H H)
Family 5: (T T T)	Family 10: (H T H)

4. The chance that it will rain in the town where a family is spending vacation is 60% for each of 3 days. A spinner is used to simulate the weather pattern over the 3-day period. There are 5 equal sized sections. 3 sections are labeled "R" to represent days with rain. 2 sections are labeled "N" to represent days with no rain. The results of the simulation are recorded below.

   (R, N, R) (N, N, R) (R, R, R) (N, R, R) (N, R, N) (R, R, N) (N, R, N) (R, N, R)

   What is the experimental probability that it will rain exactly 1 out of the 3 days?

5. **Higher Order Thinking** Of all listeners who call the local radio station on the telephone, 60% are between the ages of 15 and 25. A random number generator is used to simulate 20 groups representing the next 6 listeners who will call the radio station, and the simulated data is recorded below.

(2, 3, 5, 9, 1, 6)	(2, 0, 2, 2, 7, 2)	(9, 9, 9, 5, 5, 0)	(0, 4, 9, 9, 4, 0)	(3, 7, 7, 2, 5, 8)
(2, 5, 5, 2, 4, 1)	(6, 4, 6, 7, 9, 4)	(5, 2, 9, 7, 8, 3)	(4, 7, 1, 3, 4, 3)	(7, 0, 7, 3, 3, 5)
(8, 6, 3, 0, 0, 6)	(9, 1, 0, 7, 7, 7)	(2, 6, 3, 1, 1, 7)	(8, 0, 0, 8, 3, 7)	(9, 1, 8, 7, 4, 6)
(9, 3, 6, 0, 5, 0)	(0, 0, 8, 3, 7, 8)	(2, 5, 2, 7, 3, 5)	(3, 5, 1, 5, 0, 2)	(5, 1, 9, 9, 7, 4)

a. Which of the following describes possible numbers that may be used to represent listeners within and outside of the age range?

   Ⓐ Within Age Range: 0 through 5   Outside of Age Range: 6 through 10

   Ⓑ Within Age Range: 0 through 4   Outside of Age Range: 5 through 9

   Ⓒ Within Age Range: 0 through 6   Outside of Age Range: 7 through 9

   Ⓓ Within Age Range: 0 through 5   Outside of Age Range: 6 through 9

b. Based on the simulated data, what is the probability that the next six listeners that call the radio station are between 15 and 25 years of age?

c. How will the simulated results change if a different set of numbers are assigned to conduct this simulation? Explain.

☑ Assessment Practice

6. The probability that the Mustangs win a certain game is 50%. A fair coin is used to simulate the team's chance of winning 4 of the next 7 games. A winning game is represented by a coin that lands heads up.

   H, H, T, T, H, T, T   H, T, T, H, H, H, T   T, T, H, T, H, T, T

   H, T, H, H, H, T, T   T, T, H, H, H, T, H   H, T, H, T, T, H, H

PART A

Based on the simulated results of the 6 trials above, what is the probability that the Mustangs will win 4 of the next 7 games?

PART B

According to the simulated results, what is the probability that the Mustangs win 4 games before playing all 7 games?

Name: _____

10-1 Additional Practice

1. What is the actual length of the truck?

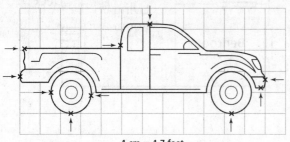

1 cm = 1.7 feet
The gridlines are spaced 1 cm apart.

2. A portion of a map with cities A and B is shown. The map uses a scale of 1 inch to 30 miles. A new map has a scale of 2 inches = 15 miles. How far apart are cities A and B on the new map?

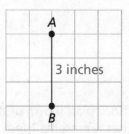

3. A 12-foot wall measures 2.5 inches on a scale drawing. In the drawing, a second wall is 9 inches long. What is the actual length of the second wall?

4. In a scale drawing, the length of a rectangular room is 6 inches, and the width is 3 inches. The actual length of the room is 18 feet.

   a. What is the scale of the drawing?

   b. In a new scale drawing of the same room, the length of the room measures 4 inches. What is the scale of the new drawing? Explain.

5. On a scale drawing of a fence, 3.75 inches represent 24 feet.

   What is the actual length of a fence that is 2.8 inches long in the drawing?

6. Higher Order Thinking If carpet costs $1.50 per square foot including the cost of installation, how much will it cost to carpet the entire living room floor of the cabin shown at the right?

The gridlines are spaced 1 cm apart.
1 cm = 4 feet

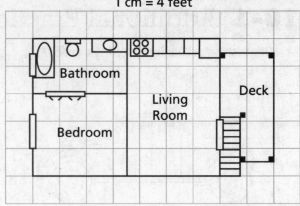

7. On the floor plan shown at the right, 1.25 inches represents 2 feet.

   a. What is the actual length of the entire floor?

   b. What is the actual area of the entire floor? Explain how you found the area.

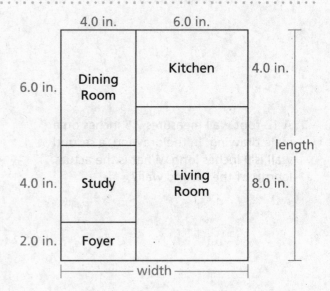

✅ Assessment Practice

8. An architect is recreating the blueprint for a deck with an existing scale factor of 1 in. = 2 ft, shown at the right. The architect is using a different scale so that the length of the deck on the new blueprint measures 8 inches.

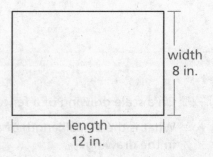

   PART A

   What is the scale factor of the new blueprint?

   1 inch = ☐ feet

   PART B

   What is the width, in inches, of the deck on the new blueprint?

10-2 Additional Practice

Scan for Multimedia

1. What quadrilateral can be drawn that has exactly two pairs of perpendicular sides?

2. What geometric shape may describe a quadrilateral that has two sides with length 8 cm and two sides with length 5 cm?

3. A four-sided sandbox has exactly two right angles, two side lengths 5 ft, and two side lengths 6 ft. What geometric shape best describes the shape of the sandbox?

4. A park has a pond shaped like a quadrilateral with all sides 18 feet long and at least one right angle. What geometric shape best describes the shape of the pond?

5. What geometric shape may describe a quadrilateral that has exactly two pairs of parallel sides and no right angles?

6. A playground is shaped like a quadrilateral with all sides 27 feet long, with two angle measures of 65° and two angle measures of 115°. What geometric shape best describes the shape of the playground?

7. Draw a quadrilateral with one angle that measures 25° and one pair of parallel sides, with the shorter parallel side measuring exactly 5 units in length.

8. Use computer drawing software to construct a quadrilateral with two pairs of parallel sides and two angles measuring 125°. What geometric shape describes this quadrilateral?

9. **Higher Order Thinking** Draw a quadrilateral using geometry software with all sides 2 units long and at least one angle that measures 40°. What is the specific name of the quadrilateral?

✅ Assessment Practice

10. Rachel correctly constructs a quadrilateral given the following conditions.

    Two sides measure 2 units in length. Two sides measure 3 units in length. The figure has 2 lines of symmetry.

    Which quadrilateral does Rachel construct?

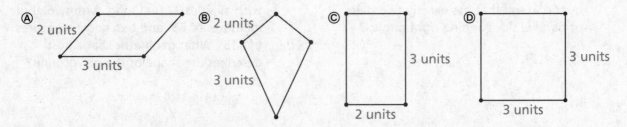

Ⓐ 2 units / 3 units

Ⓑ 2 units / 3 units

Ⓒ 3 units / 2 units

Ⓓ 3 units / 3 units

11. Draw a quadrilateral that has exactly one pair of parallel sides, with the longer parallel side having a length of 10 units, and the shorter parallel side having a length of 6 units. Make the non-parallel sides equal in length to one another. What is the name of the quadrilateral that you constructed?

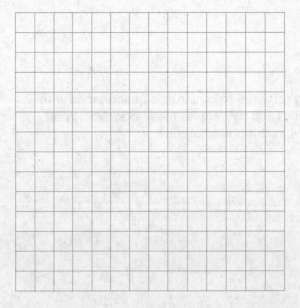

10-3 Additional Practice

1. How many triangles can be drawn with side lengths of 3 units, 4 units, and 5 units? Explain.

2. Draw a triangle with side lengths of 16 units and 30 units and an included angle of 90°.

3. How many triangles can be drawn with one 90° angle, a 70° angle, and an included side measuring 3 inches? Explain.

4. **Critique Reasoning** Dora says that only one triangle can be constructed with two given side lengths and one given angle measure. Is Dora correct? Explain.

5. Can a triangle be drawn with side lengths of 7.3 meters, 4.6 meters, and 11 meters? Explain.

6. Danielle wants to construct different triangles with angle measures of 90°, 45°, and 45°, but she was only able to draw the triangle shown at the right.

   What mistake might Danielle have made?

7. Draw two different triangles given the following conditions for ∠TRI:

TR = 6 units, IT = 9 units, m∠TIR = 35°

8. In △NMP, m∠MNP = 45°, MN = 7.5 feet, and MP = 5 feet.

How many triangles can be drawn when given the information above?

9. Higher Order Thinking Given two angle measures and the length of the included side, does this side length affect the number of triangles that can be drawn? Explain.

✓ Assessment Practice

10. Which of the following describes possible methods that can be used to construct a triangle given the lengths of two sides and the measure of a nonincluded angle? Select all that apply.

☐ Construct one side with a given length. Use this side to form an angle with the given measure, then construct the opposite side with the given length.

☐ Construct one side with a given length. Use this side to form an angle with the given measure, then extend the other side of the angle until it has the same measure as the other given length and construct the side opposite the angle.

☐ Construct an angle with the given measure. Extend each side of the angle until these sides have the same measure as the given lengths and construct the side opposite the angle.

☐ Construct an angle with the given measure. Extend one side of the angle until it has the same measure as one of the given lengths and draw the side opposite the angle with the given length.

☐ Construct an angle with the given measure. Extend one side of the angle until it has the same measure as one of the given lengths. At the end of the extended side length, construct a side with a 90° angle that has the same length as the other given side length. Then extend the other side with the included angle until it forms a triangle.

10-4 Additional Practice

1. a. Name a pair of adjacent angles in this figure.

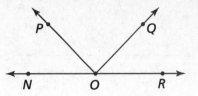

b. What common point is shared by all adjacent angles in this figure?

---

2. Dexter needs to find each angle in this figure that is adjacent to ∠LON. He claims that ∠MON is adjacent to ∠LON.

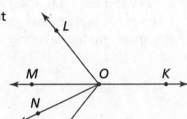

a. List each angle that is adjacent to ∠LON.

b. Why is Dexter's claim incorrect?

---

3. a. Use vertical angles to find the value of x.

b. Explain how to find the value of x without using vertical angles.

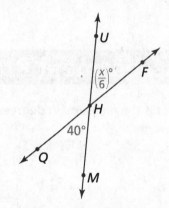

(The figure is not shown to scale.)

---

4. Find the measure of the complement to an 18° angle. Explain your answer.

---

5. The measure of ∠1 is 39°. What is the measure of the angle adjacent to ∠1? Explain.

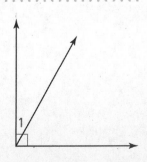

6. The adjacent angles shown below are supplementary. Find the value of x.

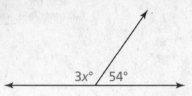

$3x°$ $54°$

7. Find the supplementary angle to an angle that is 128.9°. Explain your answer.

8. **Higher Order Thinking** In the diagram, $m\angle1 = (125 - y)°$, $m\angle2 = 24°$, and $m\angle3 = (x + 46)°$. Solve for x and y and find $m\angle1$ and $m\angle3$. Explain how you found the measure of each angle and the value of each variable.

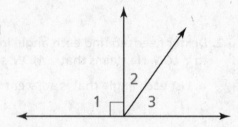

2
1 3

☑ Assessment Practice

9. What is the measure, in degrees, of angle b?

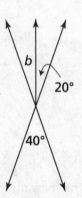

b
20°
40°

10. What is the measure, in degrees, of the highlighted angle?

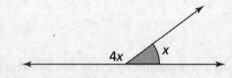

$4x$ x

10-5 Additional Practice

Scan for Multimedia

1. a. The circumference of a circle measures 11.27π ft. What is the measure of the diameter of this circle?

2. Circle A has a radius of 21 meters. Circle B has a radius of 28 meters.

    a. Find the circumference of each circle in terms of π.

    b. Reasoning Is the relationship between the radius and circumference the same for all circles? Explain.

3. The diameter of a circle is 18 m. Eugene claims that the circumference of the circle is about 113.04 m.

    a. What is the circumference of the circle? Use 3.14 for π.

    b. What mistake did Eugene likely make?

4. How much fencing is required to enclose a circular garden whose radius is 14 m? Use $\frac{22}{7}$ for π.

5. What is the diameter of a circle with a circumference of 132 ft? Use $\frac{22}{7}$ for π.

6. How many flowers, spaced every 4 inches, are needed to surround a circular garden with a 200 inch radius? Use 3.14 for π.

7. Wheel A has a diameter of 25.4 inches. Wheel B has a diameter of 22.5 inches.

About how much farther will Wheel A travel in one rotation than Wheel B?
Use 3.14 for π. Round your answer to the nearest whole number.

. . . .

8. Find the circumference of the circle at the right
in terms of π.

13 mi

✓ Assessment Practice

9. Circle Y has a radius of 22 meters and Circle Z has a radius of 27 meters.
Which of the following statements are true? Select all that apply.

☐ The circumference of Circle Y = 44 π m

☐ The circumference of Circle Z = 27 π m

☐ The circumference of Circle Y is approximately
32 m less than the circumference of Circle Z.

☐ The circumference of Circle Z is approximately 170 m.

☐ The circumference of Circle Z is approximately
32 m less than the circumference of Circle Y.

10. The circumference of one coin is 8.03 cm. The circumference of
another coin is 0.33 cm smaller.

a. What is the first step to find the diameter of the smaller coin?

Ⓐ Find the radius of the smaller coin.

Ⓑ Find the diameter of the larger coin.

Ⓒ Find the circumference of the larger coin.

Ⓓ Find the circumference of the smaller coin.

b. Find the diameter of the smaller coin.
Use $\frac{22}{7}$ for π.

10-6 Additional Practice

1. A certain coin is a circle with diameter 18 mm. What is the exact area of either face of the coin in terms of π?

2. The radius of a circular sign is 12 inches. Equal parts of the sign are painted red and yellow. How many square inches are painted each color? Use 3.14 for π.

3. A water sprinkler sprays water outward in a circular pattern. What area will be watered if the radius of the spray from the sprinkler is 18 ft? Write an exact answer in terms of π.

4. How many times greater is the area of Circle 1 than the area of Circle 2? Explain your answer.

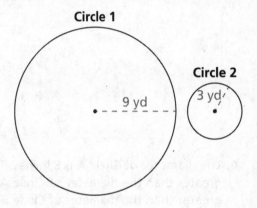

Circle 1

Circle 2

9 yd

3 yd

5. a. The diameter of Circle J is 18 cm. The diameter of Circle K is 31 cm. Which circle has the greater area and by how much? Use 3.14 for π.

   b. Describe how you can compare the areas of two circles.

6. **Higher Order Thinking** Sandra just finished planting avacados, carrots, radishes, tomatoes, and spinach in her new garden. The garden is a circle whose diameter is 50 yards. If she planted equal regions of each vegetable, what is the area of Sandra's garden that has carrots? Use 3.14 for π.

7. The circumference of a circular patio is 53.38 feet. What is the area of the patio? Use 3.14 for an approximation for π. Round to the nearest tenth.

8. The area of a circular window is 113.04 square inches. What is the diameter of the window? Use 3.14 for π.

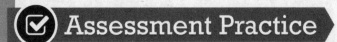

✓ Assessment Practice

9. The figure is made by attaching semicircles to each side of an 11 ft-by-11-ft square. Find the area, in square feet, enclosed by the figure. Use 3.14 for π. Round to the nearest whole number.

11 ft

10. The diameter of Circle A is 8 inches. The diameter of Circle B is 4 inches greater than the diameter of Circle A. The diameter of Circle C is 4 inches greater than the diameter of Circle B.

PART A

What is the area, in square inches, of Circle C? Use 3.14 for π.

PART B

How many times greater is the area of Circle C than the area of Circle A?

Name: _____

10-7 Additional Practice

1. What are the dimensions of the vertical cross section that is parallel to the right and left faces of the right rectangular prism?

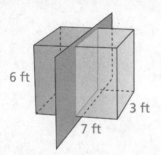

6 ft

3 ft

7 ft

2. Look for Relationships The horizontal cross section shown is parallel to the base of the pyramid. If the shortest side of the cross section measures 1.2 cm, what is the measure of the cross section's longest side? Explain.

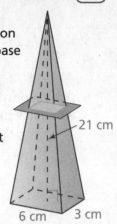

21 cm

6 cm   3 cm

3. Make Sense and Persevere A right rectangular prism has a length of 104 inches, a width of 66 inches, and height of 54 inches. What are the dimensions of a horizontal cross section of the prism?

4. What is a good description of the cross section shown that is parallel to the edge of the prism that measures 5 millimeters.

16 mm

12 mm   5 mm

5. A right pyramid is 18 cm tall and has a rectangular base that is 9 cm long and 3 cm wide. Describe the cross section formed when a plane parallel to the base of the pyramid intersects the pyramid between its base and the vertex opposite its base.

6. Make Sense and Persevere Describe the vertical cross section that intersects the top vertex and is parallel to the edges measuring 17 m of the right pyramid shown.

13 m

17 m   7 m

7. A 0.75 inch thick slice is cut from a stick of butter as shown.

Draw the cross section of this slice and then find its area.

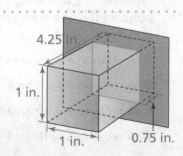

4.25 in.

1 in.

1 in.   0.75 in.

8. Use the figure at the right.

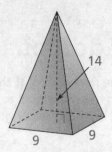

   a. How can the rectangular pyramid shown be sliced to form two identical solid figures?

   b. Draw a possible cross section of the pyramid when it is cut into two identical pieces

   c. What is the area of the cross section?

---

9. Reasoning Explain why there can be two vertical cross sections for a right rectangular prism but only one horizontal cross section when the slices are made parallel to a side.

10. Higher Order Thinking Two vertical cross sections of an unknown rectangular prism are given. One vertical cross section is parallel to a pair of faces of the prism. The other cross section is parallel to a different pair of faces of the prism. Can the entire prism be drawn using the given cross sections? Explain.

☑ Assessment Practice

11. Which of the following may describe a cross section formed by a horizontal plane above the base that intersects the faces of the pyramid shown?

   Ⓐ A rectangle with area 90 square feet

   Ⓑ A rectangle with area 160 square feet

   Ⓒ A rectangle with area 180 square feet

   Ⓓ A rectangle with area 360 square feet

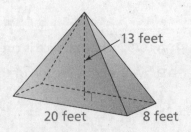

Name: _____

10-8 Additional Practice

Leveled Practice In **1–3**, find the area of the shaded parts.

1. Lucas is planting grass on the shaded portions of the yard. What will be the total area covered by grass?

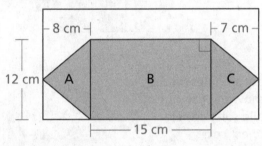

Part A = ☐ = ☐ ft²

Part B = ½ · ☐ = ☐ ft²

Part C = ½ · ☐ = ☐ ft²

Total area = ☐ ft² + ☐ ft² + ☐ ft²

= ☐ ft²

2. What is the total shaded area of the figure below?

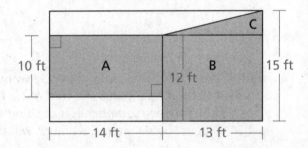

Part A = ½ · ☐ = ☐ cm²

Part B = ☐ = ☐ cm²

Part C = ½ · ☐ = ☐ cm²

Total shaded area = ☐ cm²

3. What is the total area of the shaded portion shown below?

Part A = ☐ = ☐ ft²

Part B = ☐ = ☐ ft²

Part C = ½ · ☐ = ☐ ft²

Total shaded area = ☐ ft²

4. The block of wood shown at the right is a triangular prism. What is its surface area?

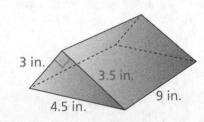

3 in.

3.5 in.

9 in.

4.5 in.

5. **Make Sense and Persevere** The bottom part of this block is a rectangular prism. The top part is a rectangular pyramid. Kiran wants to cover the block entirely with paper. How much paper does she need?

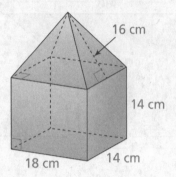

16 cm

14 cm

14 cm

18 cm

6. Find the surface area of the regular hexagonal prism shown below.

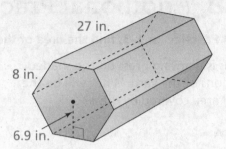

27 in.

8 in.

6.9 in.

7. The height of the rectangular prism measures 64 cm. If the height is increased by 1.5 cm, by how much will the surface area of the box increase?

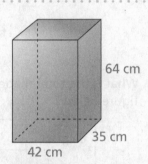

64 cm

35 cm

42 cm

8. **Higher Order Thinking** Joseph's uncle wants to put shingles on the outside walls and solar panel the roof of his barn shown at the right. It costs $2.50 for each square meter of shingles, while solar panels cost $4.00 per square meter. How much will this project cost?

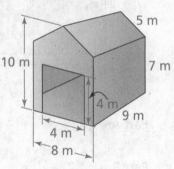

5 m

10 m

7 m

4 m

9 m

4 m

8 m

✅ Assessment Practice

9. The base of the prism shown is an isosceles triangle. What is the surface area, in square centimeters, of this prism?

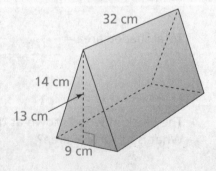

32 cm

14 cm

13 cm

9 cm

Name: _____

  PRACTICE TUTORIAL

Scan for
Multimedia

1. Find the volume of
the cube shown at
the right.

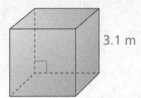

3.1 m

2. Find the volume of
the triangular
prism shown.

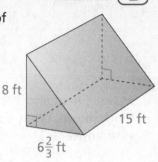

8 ft

15 ft

$6\frac{2}{3}$ ft

3. Find the volume of the hexagonal prism shown at the right.
Round to the nearest hundredth.

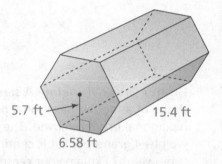

5.7 ft

15.4 ft

6.58 ft

4. The walls of an empty grain silo form a hexagonal prism
as shown at the right. Can the farmer store 4,250 cubic feet
of grain inside the silo? Explain.

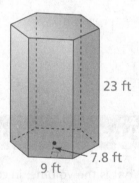

23 ft

7.8 ft

9 ft

5. A rain gutter attached to the edge of a roof
has the shape of a rectangular prism.
It is 18 feet long and 7 inches high. It has
a volume of 7,560 cubic inches. How wide
is the gutter?

6. Make Sense and Persevere A baker
makes a layered cake with two layers
that are rectangular prisms. Each layer
is 2 inches tall. What is the volume
of the cake?

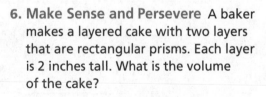

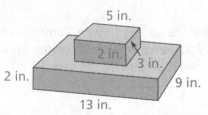

5 in.

2 in.

3 in.

2 in.

9 in.

13 in.

7. The triangular prism shown at the right has two bases that are equilateral triangles. The perimeter of each base measures 63 cm. What is the volume of the prism?

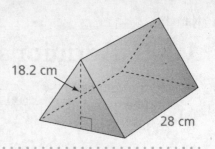

18.2 cm

28 cm

8. Make Sense and Persevere Morgan made the display block shown. What is the volume of the block? Explain your answer.

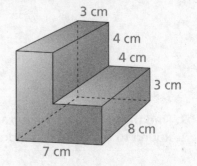

3 cm

4 cm

4 cm

3 cm

8 cm

7 cm

9. Higher Order Thinking A steel tube is constructed in the shape of a regular hexagonal prism with a smaller regular hexagonal prism removed. The material used for the tube weighs 4 grams per cubic centimeter. How much does the tube weigh? Explain your reasoning.

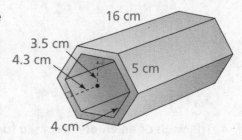

16 cm

3.5 cm

4.3 cm

5 cm

4 cm

10. What is the volume, in cubic inches, of the triangular prism shown at the right?

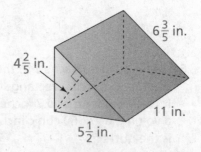

$6\frac{3}{5}$ in.

$4\frac{2}{5}$ in.

11 in.

$5\frac{1}{2}$ in.

11. Before adding flowers, James fills the vase shown $\frac{1}{3}$ full with water. How much water, in cubic centimeters, does it take to fill the vase $\frac{1}{3}$ full?

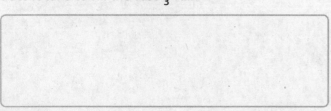

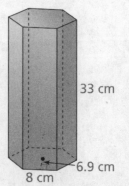

33 cm

6.9 cm

8 cm

Name: _____

11-1 Additional Practice

Scan for
Multimedia

1. Graph $D'E'F'$, the image of triangle DEF after a translation 1 unit right and 3 units down.

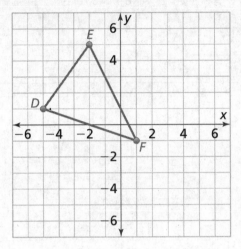

2. The coordinates of $\triangle DEF$ are $D(4, 3)$, $E(7, 3)$, and $F(6, 8)$. If you translate $\triangle DEF$ 4 units left and 3 units up, what are the coordinates of F?

3. Quadrilateral $Q'R'S'T'$ is the image of quadrilateral $QRST$ after a translation.

   a. If the perimeter of $QRST$ is about 12.4 units, what is the perimeter of $Q'R'S'T'$?

   b. If $m\angle S = 115°$, what is $m\angle S'$?

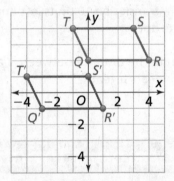

4. Quadrilateral $W'X'Y'Z'$ is a translation of quadrilateral $WXYZ$. Describe the translation.

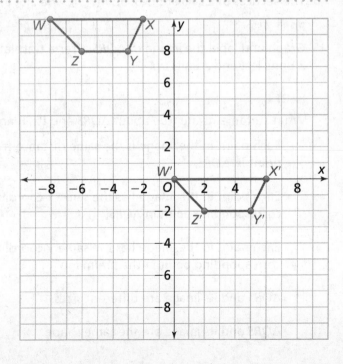

11-1 Analyze Translations **153**

5. Is △J'K'L' a translation of △JKL Explain.

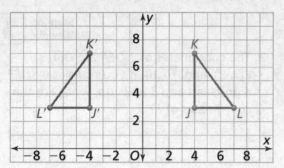

6. Quadrilateral G'R'A'M' is a translation of quadrilateral GRAM. Describe the translation.

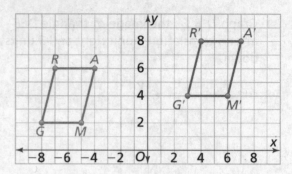

7. Higher Order Thinking The vertices of pentagon VWXYZ are V(4, 5), W(6, 5), X(6, 7), Y(5, 8), and Z(4, 7).

   a. Draw VWXYZ and V'W'X'Y'Z', its image after a translation 10 units left and 2 units down.

   b. Estimate the distance between V and V' to the nearest tenth.

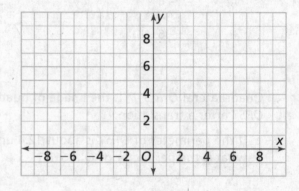

Assessment Practice

8. The vertices of △QRS are Q(3, 3), R(7, 3), and S(5, 8).

PART A

Graph and label the image of △QRS after a translation 2 units left and 2 units up.

PART B

What statements are true about △QRS and its image?

☐ Each point in the image is the same distance from each point in △QRS.

☐ Each point in the image has the same x-coordinate as the corresponding point in △QRS.

☐ Each point in the image has the same y-coordinate as the corresponding point in the preimage.

☐ △QRS and its image are different sizes.

☐ △QRS and its image are the same shape.

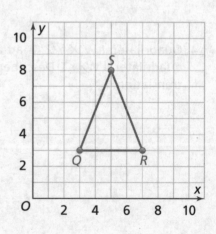

Name: _____

11-2 Additional Practice

1. Leveled Practice Rectangle *ABCD* is shown. Draw the reflection of rectangle *ABCD* across the *y*-axis.

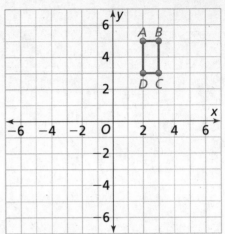

Identify the points of the pre-image.

Identify the points of the image.

A [ ]   A′ [ ]

B [ ]   B′ [ ]

C [ ]   C′ [ ]

D [ ]   D′ [ ]

Plot the points and draw rectangle *A′B′C′D′*.

2. Reasoning Is △*E′F′G′* a reflection of △*EFG* across the line? Explain.

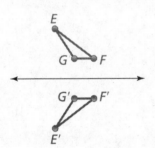

3. Consider the graph of △*ABC* and its image △*A′B′C′*. What reflection produces this image?

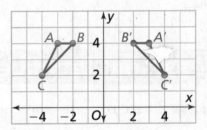

4. △*A′B′C′* is an image of △*ABC*.

a. How do the *x*-coordinates of the vertices change?

b. How do the *y*-coordinates of the vertices change?

c. What reflection produces the image?

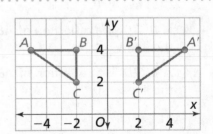

5. The vertices of △ABC are A(−5, 4), B(−2, 4), and C(−4, 2). If △ABC is reflected across the y-axis, find the coordinates of the vertex C′.

6. △E′F′G′ is the image of △EFG. What reflection produces this image?

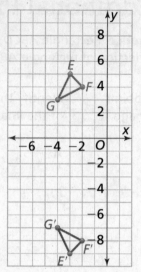

7. Higher Order Thinking The vertices of △ABC are A(−5, 5), B(−2, 4), and C(−4, 2). △ABC is reflected across the y-axis and then reflected again across the x-axis to produce the image △A′B′C′. What are the coordinates of △A′B′C′?

☑ Assessment Practice

8. Quadrilateral △A′B′C′D′ is an image of quadrilateral ABCD.

PART A

What reflection produces this image?

Ⓐ A′B′C′D′ is a reflection of ABCD across the line x = 1.

Ⓑ A′B′C′D′ is a reflection of ABCD across the line y = 0.

Ⓒ A′B′C′D′ is a reflection of ABCD across the line y = 1.

Ⓓ A′B′C′D′ is a reflection of ABCD across the line x = 0.

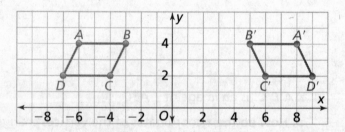

PART B

If m∠A = 110°, what is m∠A′?

Name: _____

11-3 Additional Practice

1. Leveled Practice What is the angle of rotation about the origin that maps △PQR to △P'Q'R'?

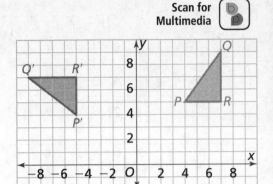

2. Is △X'Y'Z' a rotation of △XYZ? Explain.

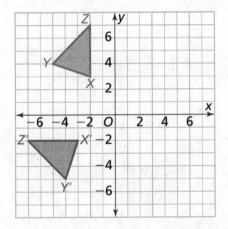

3. What is the angle of rotation about the origin that maps quadrilateral PQRS to quadrilateral P'Q'R'S'?

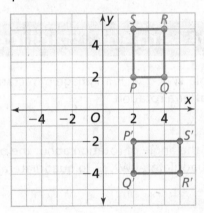

4. Pentagon JKLMN is rotated 180° about the origin. Graph and label the coordinates of pentagon J'K'L'M'N'.

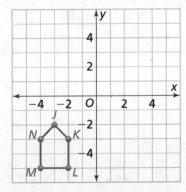

5. Is △P'Q'R' a 90° rotation of △PQR about the origin? Explain.

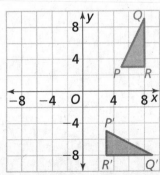

6. △TRI is rotated 270° about the origin. Graph and label the coordinates of △T′R′I′.

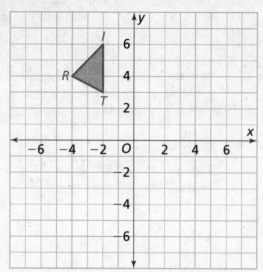

7. **Higher Order Thinking** Point N has coordinates (3, 4). On a quiz yesterday, Ari incorrectly claimed that if you rotate N 180° about the origin, the coordinates of N′ are (−4, 3). What are the correct coordinates for N′? What was Ari's likely error?

☑ Assessment Practice

8. Rectangle W′X′Y′Z′ is an image of rectangle WXYZ after a rotation.

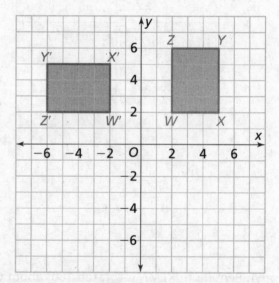

PART A

What is the angle of rotation about the origin that maps quadrilateral WXYZ to quadrilateral W′X′Y′Z′?

Ⓐ 90°

Ⓑ 180°

Ⓒ 270°

Ⓓ 360°

PART B

What changed when mapping quadrilateral WXYZ to quadrilateral W′X′Y′Z′?

Ⓐ size

Ⓑ shape

Ⓒ position

Ⓓ orientation

Name: _____

11-4 Additional Practice

1. Leveled Practice Describe a sequence of transformations that maps △EFG to △MNO.

A translation [ ] units left and [ ]

units down, followed by a [ ]

across the [ ]

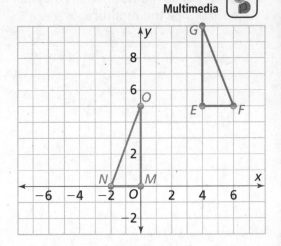

2. △D′E′F′ is an image of △DEF after a sequence of transformations.

a. Describe a sequence of transformations that maps △DEF to △D′E′F′.

b. Describe another way that you could map △DEF to △D′E′F′.

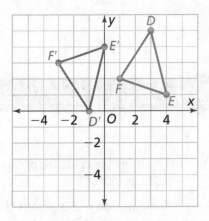

3. Map quadrilateral ABCD to quadrilateral A′B′C′D′ with a rotation of 180° about the origin followed by a translation 3 units left and 7 units up.

4. Describe a sequence of transformations that maps △XYZ to △X′Y′Z′.

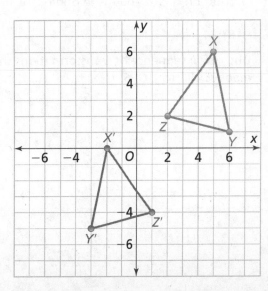

5. Higher Order Thinking A small store is rearranging their furniture. Describe the sequences of transformations they can use to rearrange the furniture.

6. Map quadrilateral *ABCD* to quadrilateral *HIJK* with a reflection across the *x*-axis followed by a translation 4 units left and 2 units down.

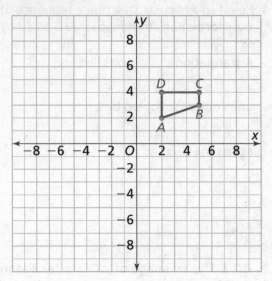

7. PART A

Which sequence of transformations maps △*QRS* to △*ABC*?

Ⓐ A rotation of 90° about the origin, followed by a translation 3 units left.

Ⓑ A reflection across the *x*-axis, followed by a rotation of 90° about the origin.

Ⓒ A rotation of 90° about the origin, followed by a reflection across the *y*-axis.

Ⓓ A reflection across the *x*-axis, followed by a rotation of 90° about the origin.

PART B

Describe a sequence of transformations that maps △*ABC* to △*QRS*.

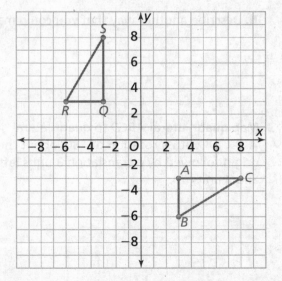

11-5 Additional Practice

1. Leveled Practice △D'E'F' is the image of △DEF after a reflection across the *x*-axis and a translation 6 units left and 6 units up. Is the image the same size and shape as the pre-image? Explain.

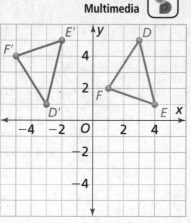

A reflection [   ] change the size and shape of the figure.

A translation [   ] change the size and shape of the figure.

△DEF and △D'E'F' [   ] the same size and shape.

2. Which two triangles are congruent? Describe a sequence of transformations that maps one figure onto the other.

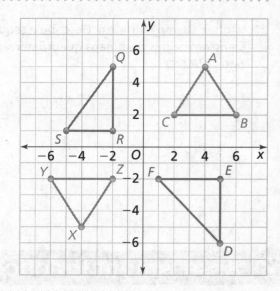

3. Is *ABCD* ≅ *A'B'C'D'*? Explain.

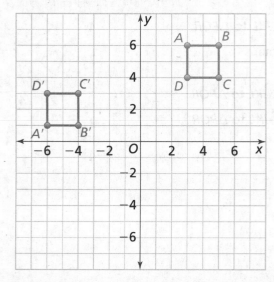

4. Construct Arguments Describe a way to show △DEF is congruent to △D'E'F'.

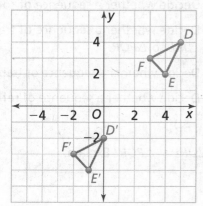

5. How can you decide if △DEF ≅ △D′E′F′?

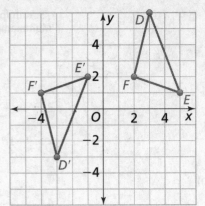

6. Is ABCDE ≅ VWXYZ? Explain.

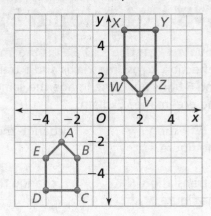

7. Higher Order Thinking Describe a sequence of transformations that maps quadrilateral ABCD onto A′B′C′D′.

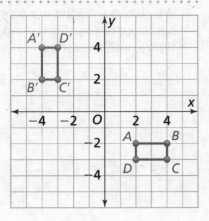

Assessment Practice

8. PART A

How can you determine whether △JKL ≅ △PQR?

Ⓐ Decide whether a sequence of rotations maps △JKL to △PQR.

Ⓑ Decide whether a sequence of transformations maps △JKL to △PQR.

Ⓒ Decide whether a sequence of translations maps △JKL to △PQR.

Ⓓ Decide whether a sequence of reflections maps △JKL to △PQR.

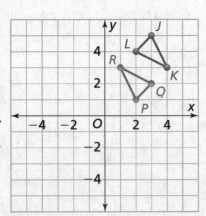

PART B

Is △JKL ≅ △PQR? Explain.

Name: _____

11-6 Additional Practice

1. Leveled Practice Draw the image of
△*ABC* after a dilation with center (0, 0)
and scale factor $\frac{1}{4}$.

Find the coordinates of each point in the
original figure.

A: (☐), (☐)

B: (☐), (☐)

C: (☐), (☐)

Multiply each coordinate by ☐.

Find the coordinates of each point in
the image:

A′: (☐), (☐)

B′: (☐), (☐)

C′: (☐), (☐)

Graph the image.

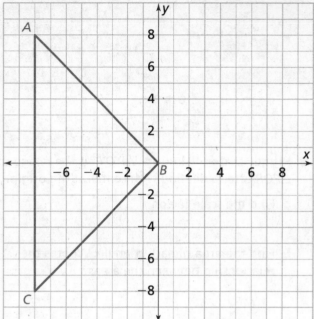

2. △*RST* has vertices *R*(0, 0), *S*(6, 3), and
T(3, −3). △*R′S′T′* is the image of △*RST* after
a dilation with center (0, 0) and scale factor
$\frac{1}{3}$. What are the coordinates of point *S′*?

3. Rectangle *QUAD* has coordinates *Q*(4, 5),
U(4, 10), *A*(11, 10), and *D*(11, 5). *Q′U′A′D′*
is the image of *QUAD* after a dilation with
center (0, 0) and scale factor 5. What is the
length of segment *Q′U′*?

4. The graph shows △*KJL* and △*K′J′L′*, its image
after a dilation.

a. Is this dilation an enlargement or a reduction?
Explain.

b. Find the scale factor of the dilation.

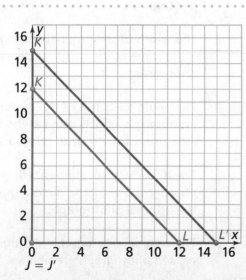

5. Draw the image of △PQR after a dilation with center (0, 0) and scale factor 3.

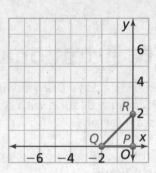

6. Higher Order Thinking △P'Q'R' is the image of △PQR after a dilation with center at the origin.

a. Find the scale factor.

b. Find the area of each triangle. What is the relationship between the areas?

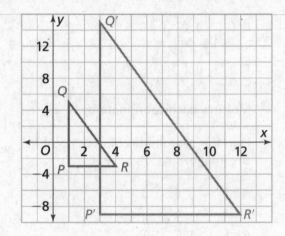

7. A photographer uses a computer program to resize a photograph by a scale factor of $\frac{2}{3}$. What is true about the resized photograph? Select all that apply.

☐ The length of the original photograph is the same as the length of the resized photograph.

☐ The width of the original photograph is the same as the width of the resized photograph.

☐ The angle measures of the original photograph are the same as the angle measures of the resized photograph.

☐ The dimensions of the resized photograph are $\frac{2}{3}$ the dimensions of the original photograph.

☐ The original photograph and the resized photograph are similar.

8. Is the dilation an enlargement or a reduction? Explain.

11-7 Additional Practice

1. **Leveled Practice** *ABCD* and *EFGH* are quadrilaterals. Given *ABCD* ~ *EFGH*, describe a sequence of transformations that maps *ABCD* to *EFGH*

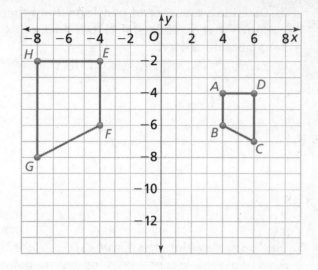

- Reflection across the ☐

- Translation ☐ unit(s) right

  and ☐ unit(s) up

- Dilation with center (0, 0) and scale

  factor ☐

2. a. If △*PQR* were similar to △*XYZ*, what angle would correspond to ∠*Q*?

   b. Are the triangles similar? Explain.

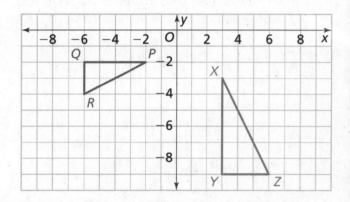

3. Quadrilateral *RSTU* is translated 6 units right and 4 units up, and then dilated with center of dilation (0, 0) and scale factor $\frac{1}{2}$. Graph the resulting similar quadrilateral *VXYZ*.

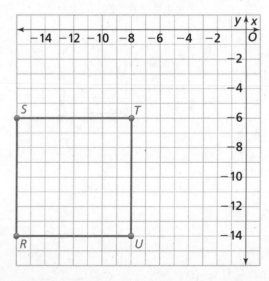

4. Describe a sequence of transformations that shows that △*NOP* is similar to △*QRS*.

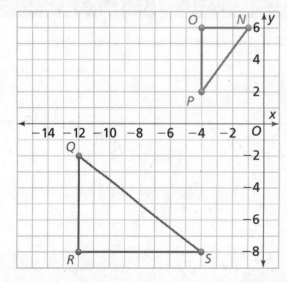

5. Quadrilateral *RSTU* ~ quadrilateral *VXYZ*.

   a. Which angle corresponds to ∠S?

   b. Describe a sequence of transformations that shows that quadrilateral *RSTU* is similar to quadrilateral *VXYZ*.

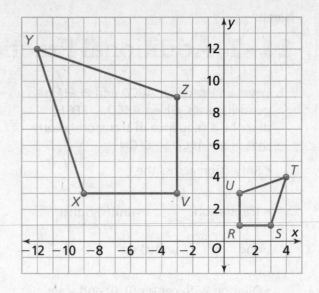

6. **Higher Order Thinking** Given △*JKL* ~ △*XYZ*. Find two possible coordinates for missing point *Y*. For each coordinate chosen, describe a sequence of transformations that could map △*JKL* to △*XYZ*.

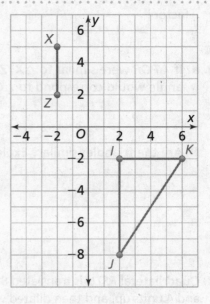

✅ Assessment Practice

7. Are quadrilaterals *RSTU* and *VXYZ* similar? Explain.

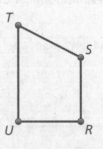

11-8 Additional Practice

Scan for
Multimedia

1. Leveled Practice If $p \| q$, what is the value of v?

∠u and ∠v are [_____] angles.

So, ∠u and ∠v are [_____].

$m\angle v$ is [_____].

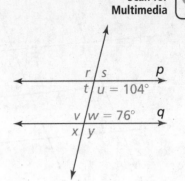

---

2. Are ∠6 and ∠7 corresponding angles if $a \| b$ and $c \| d$? Explain.

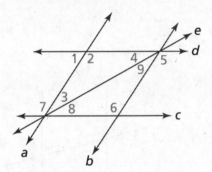

3. Find $m\angle v$ given that $p \| q$, $m\angle u = 75.8°$, and $m\angle w = 104.2°$.

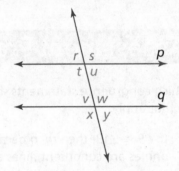

---

4. In the figure $m \| n$. What is the value of x?

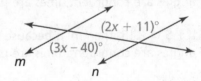

---

5. Reasoning What value of x will show that line m is parallel to line n? Explain.

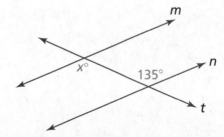

6. Higher Order Thinking Determine which lines, if any, in the figure are parallel.

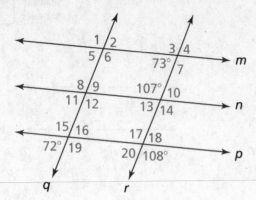

7. In the figure $d \parallel m$. What is the value of x?

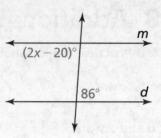

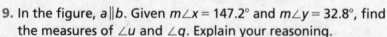

8. Which congruence statements show that $m \parallel n$? Select all that apply.

☐ If $\angle 9 \cong \angle 13$, then $m \parallel n$ because if corresponding angles are congruent, lines are parallel.

☐ If $\angle 4 \cong \angle 5$, then $m \parallel n$ because if alternate interior angles are congruent, lines are parallel.

☐ If $\angle 12 \cong \angle 13$, then $m \parallel n$ because if alternate interior angles are congruent, lines are parallel.

☐ If $\angle 5 \cong \angle 15$, then $m \parallel n$ because if corresponding angles are congruent, lines are parallel.

☐ If $\angle 10 \cong \angle 14$, then $m \parallel n$ because if alternate interior angles are congruent, lines are parallel.

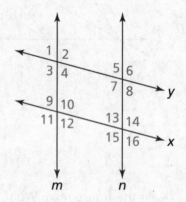

9. In the figure, $a \parallel b$. Given $m\angle x = 147.2°$ and $m\angle y = 32.8°$, find the measures of $\angle u$ and $\angle q$. Explain your reasoning.

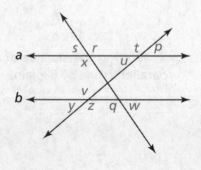

11-9 Additional Practice

1. Leveled Practice For the figure shown, find $m\angle 1$.

$\angle 1$ is a [_____] of the 119° angle.

The 119° angle is equal to the sum of its [_____].

So, $m\angle 1 = $ [_____] − [_____].

$m\angle 1 = $ [_____]

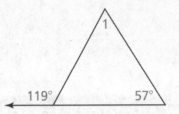

---

2. Find $m\angle B$ for the triangle shown.

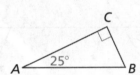

3. Find $m\angle R$.

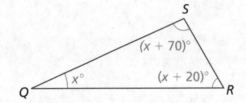

---

4. Reasoning Can you find the $m\angle 1$ without using remote interior angles? Explain.

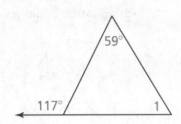

---

5. Find the value of x in the triangle.

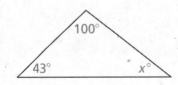

6. Higher Order Thinking Given that $m\angle A = (16x)°$, $m\angle C = (8x + 20)°$, and $m\angle D = 128°$, what is $m\angle B$?

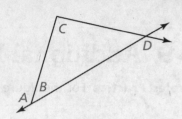

7. The measure of $\angle 6$ is 120°. The measure of $\angle 5$ is 100°. What is the measure of $\angle 4$?

Ⓐ 140

Ⓑ 80

Ⓒ 60

Ⓓ 40

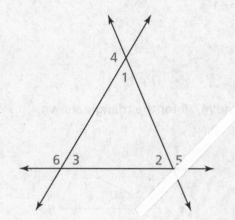

8. In the figure, $m\angle 1 = (5x + 11)°$, $m\angle 2 = (3x + 22)°$, and $m\angle 3 = (9x + 28)°$.

PART A

Which equation could you use to find $m\angle 1$?

Ⓐ $m\angle 1 + m\angle 2 + m\angle 3 = 90°$

Ⓑ $m\angle 1 + m\angle 2 + m\angle 3 = 180°$

Ⓒ $m\angle 1 - m\angle 2 = m\angle 3$

Ⓓ $m\angle 1 + m\angle 2 = m\angle 3$

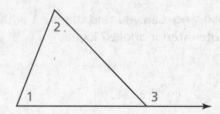

PART B

What is $m\angle 1$, in degrees?

11-10 Additional Practice

Scan for
Multimedia

1. Leveled Practice Is △XYZ ~ △XJK?

Find m∠K.

m∠K = [ ]

m∠K = [ ]

m∠K = [ ]

△XYZ and △XJK [ ] similar because

there [ ] two congruent angles.

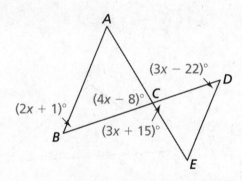

2. If △ABC and △EDC are similar, what is the value of x?

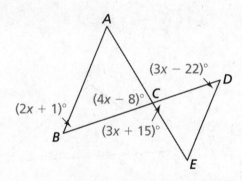

3. Is △XYZ ~ △GHI? Explain.

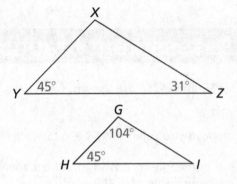

4. Construct Arguments Is △QRT ~ △GHI? Explain.

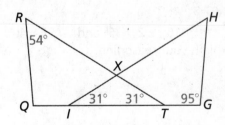

5. Is △TUV ~ △WXV? Explain.

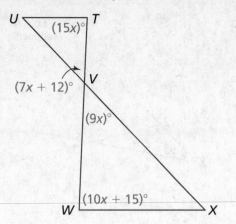

6. Higher Order Thinking Are the triangles similar? Explain.

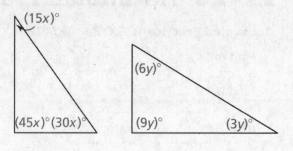

---

7. △WSR and △ZSP are shown.

PART A

How can you tell if △WSR ~ △ZSP?

Ⓐ If one angle of △WSR is half the measure of one angle of △ZSP

Ⓑ If two angles of △WSR are proportional to two angles of △ZSP

Ⓒ If two angles of △WSR are congruent to two angles of △ZSP

Ⓓ If one angle of △WSR is congruent to one angle of △ZSP

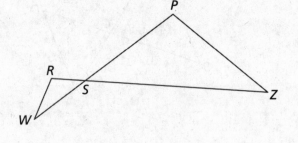

PART B

If ∠R = 110°, ∠Z = 35° and ∠PST = 40°, is △WSR ~ △ZSP? Explain your reasoning.

Name: _____

12-1 Additional Practice

PRACTICE   TUTORIAL

Leveled Practice In **1** and **2**, find the missing side length of each triangle.

1.

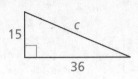

15

c

36

$$\boxed{}^2 + 36\boxed{} = c^2$$

$$\boxed{} + \boxed{} = c^2$$

$$\sqrt{\boxed{}} = \sqrt{\boxed{}}$$

$$c = \boxed{}$$

The length of the hypotenuse is $\boxed{}$ units.

2.

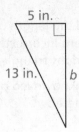

5 in.

13 in. b

$$\boxed{}^2 + b^2 = \boxed{}^2$$

$$\boxed{} + b^2 = \boxed{}$$

$$b^2 = \boxed{}$$

$$\sqrt{\boxed{}} = \sqrt{\boxed{}}$$

$$b = \boxed{}$$

The length of leg b is $\boxed{}$ inches.

3. What is the length of side a rounded to the nearest tenth of a centimeter?

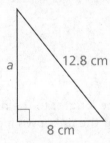

a 12.8 cm

8 cm

4. What is the length of side c rounded to the nearest tenth of an inch?

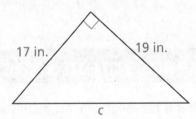

17 in.   19 in.

c

5. Two dimensions of a right triangle are 5 units and 13 units. A student writes the equation $5^2 + 13^2 = c^2$ to find the length of the third side.

a. If all the side lengths are integers, is the student's equation correct? Explain.

b. If the student is incorrect, write an equation that will give the length of the third side, and show that the equation is correct.

6. What is the length of the hypotenuse of the triangle when $x = 3$? Round your answer to the nearest tenth.

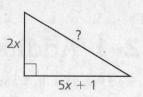
2x
?
5x + 1

7. A student was asked to find the length of the unknown leg of the right triangle. The student incorrectly said that the length of the unknown leg of the right triangle is about 6.2 centimeters.

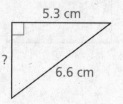
5.3 cm
?
6.6 cm

a. Find the length of the unknown leg of the right triangle to the nearest tenth of a centimeter.

b. What mistake might the student have made?

8. Higher Order Thinking Dillon places a ladder against a wall. The base of the ladder is 5 feet from the wall. The ladder is 12 feet long.

a. How high will the ladder reach?

b. How will shortening the distance between the base of the ladder and the wall affect the dimensions of the triangle they form? Explain in terms of the Pythagorean Theorem.

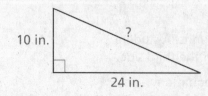
Assessment Practice

9. What is the length, in inches, of the hypotenuse of the right triangle?

10 in.
?
24 in.

10. What is the length, to the nearest tenth of a meter, of the unknown leg of the right triangle?

11 m
?
42.8 m

12-2 Additional Practice

Leveled Practice In 1 and 2, determine whether each triangle is a right triangle.

1.

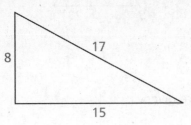

$$a^2 + b^2 = c^2$$

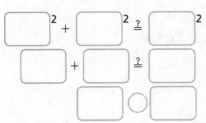

Is the triangle a right triangle? ⬜

2.

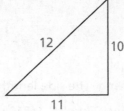

$$a^2 + b^2 = c^2$$

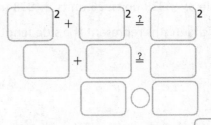

Is the triangle a right triangle? ⬜

---

3. Model with Math $\triangle LMN$ is an equilateral triangle. Is $\overline{MQ}$ the height of $\triangle LMN$? Explain.

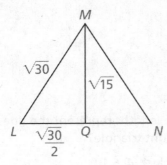

4. The side lengths of three triangles are shown. Which of the triangles are right triangles?

Triangle	Side Lengths		
1	20	$\sqrt{425}$	5
2	14	21	10
3	$\frac{6}{11}$	$\frac{8}{11}$	$\frac{10}{11}$

---

5. The length of one leg of a right triangle is 8 centimeters shorter than the hypotenuse. The hypotenuse is 42 centimeters. What is the length of the unknown leg of the right triangle rounded to the nearest tenth?

6. Model with Math △ABC is an isosceles triangle.
Is $\overline{AD}$ the height of △ABC? Explain.

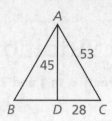

7. Higher Order Thinking The side lengths of three triangles are given.

Triangle 1: $\sqrt{519}$ units, 27 units, $\sqrt{210}$ units

Triangle 2: 21 units, $\sqrt{109}$ units, $\sqrt{420}$ units

Triangle 3: $\sqrt{338}$ units, 26 units, $\sqrt{338}$ units

a. Which lengths represent the side lengths of a right triangle? Explain.

b. For any triangles that are not right triangles, use any two of the sides to make a right triangle. Explain.

☑ Assessment Practice

8. Is △ABC a right triangle? Explain.

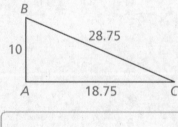

9. Which lengths represent the side lengths of a right triangle?

Triangle 1: 4, 6, 10

Triangle 2: 6, 8, 10

Triangle 3: 10, 24, 26

Ⓐ Triangle 1 and Triangle 3 are right triangles.

Ⓑ Triangle 2 and Triangle 3 are right triangles.

Ⓒ All of the triangles are right triangles.

Ⓓ None of the triangles are right triangles.

Name: _____

12-3 Additional Practice

Leveled Practice In **1** and **2**, use the Pythagorean Theorem to solve.

1. A shipping company uses an inclined conveyor belt to load and unload packages. The dock is 15 feet above the ground. The base of the conveyor belt is 40 feet from the dock. What is the length of the conveyor belt? Round to the nearest tenth of a foot.

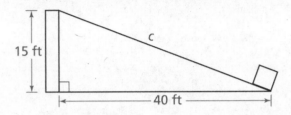

$$a^2 + b^2 = c^2$$

$$\boxed{}^2 + \boxed{}^2 = \boxed{}^2$$

$$\boxed{} + \boxed{} = \boxed{}$$

$$\boxed{} = \boxed{}$$

$$\boxed{} \approx \boxed{}$$

The length of the conveyor belt is about $\boxed{}$ feet.

2. Find the missing lengths in the rectangular prism.

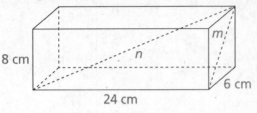

$$a^2 + b^2 = c^2$$

$$\boxed{}^2 + \boxed{}^2 = \boxed{}^2$$

$$\boxed{} + \boxed{} = \boxed{}$$

$$\boxed{} = \boxed{}$$

$$\boxed{} = \boxed{}$$

$$a^2 + b^2 = c^2$$

$$\boxed{}^2 + \boxed{}^2 = \boxed{}^2$$

$$\boxed{} + \boxed{} = \boxed{}$$

$$\boxed{} = \boxed{}$$

$$\boxed{} = \boxed{}$$

3. A square table in the cafeteria has the dimensions shown. What is the length of the diagonal of the table? Round to the nearest hundredth of a foot.

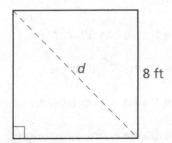

4. **Reasoning** What is the measurement of the longest line segment in a right rectangular prism that is 26 inches long, 2 inches wide, and 2 inches tall? Round to the nearest tenth of an inch.

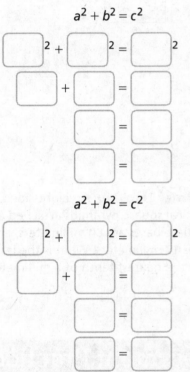

5. Make Use of Structure Li needs to find the height of the rectangular prism, x. He knows that $d = 15$ mm. If he also knows the measure of line a, can he find the measure of x? Explain.

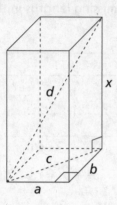

6. Sasha is building a tree house. The walls are 6.5 feet tall and she is using a brace to hold up the wall while she nails it to the floor. The brace is 8 feet long and she has positioned it 5 feet from the wall. Does her wall meet the floor at a right angle? Explain.

7. Higher Order Thinking An eight-sided game piece is shaped like two identical square pyramids attached at their bases. The perimeters of the square bases are 80 millimeters, and the slant height of each pyramid is 17 millimeters. What is the length of the game piece? Round to the nearest tenth of a millimeter.

✓ Assessment Practice

8. What are the dimensions, to the nearest meter, of the prism?

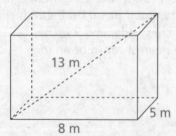

Ⓐ 5 m × 8 m × 8 m

Ⓑ 5 m × 8 m × 9 m

Ⓒ 5 m × 8 m × 10 m

Ⓓ 5 m × 8 m × 11 m

9. Carlos is making a wood picture frame. The picture frame is 11 inches by 14 inches. After nailing the frame together, Carlos measures the diagonal. If the diagonal is 19 inches long, what is true about the frame?

Ⓐ The frame has 90° corners.

Ⓑ The frame is a triangle.

Ⓒ The frame is a rectangle.

Ⓓ The frame is not a rectangle.

Name: _____

12-4 Additional Practice

1. **Leveled Practice** Use the Pythagorean Theorem to find the distance between points P and Q. Round to the nearest tenth.

Label the length, in units, of each leg of the right triangle.

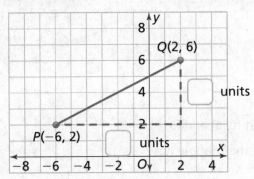

$c^2 = \boxed{}^2 + \boxed{}^2$

$c = \sqrt{\boxed{}}$

The distance between point P and point Q is about $\boxed{}$ units.

2. Find the perimeter of triangle XYZ. Round to the nearest hundredth.

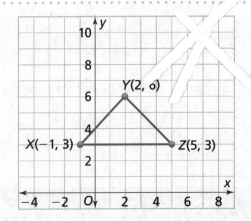

3. Determine whether the triangle is equilateral, isosceles, or scalene.

4. A shopper drives from the mall at point M to the post office located at point P. What distance does the shopper drive?

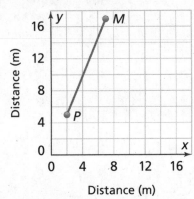

Distance (m)

5. Is point $K(10, 16)$ or point $L(12, 12)$ closer to point $J(6, 4)$? Explain.

6. Use Structure Point *B* has coordinates (−4, −2). The *x*-coordinate of point *A* is 5. The distance between point *A* and point *B* is 15 units.

a. What are the possible coordinates of point *A*?

b. Find the possible coordinates of point *A* if point *B* were moved to (−7, −2).

7. The coordinates of triangle *EFG* are *E*(28, 24), *F*(24, 27), and *G*(0, 24).

a. What is the perimeter of triangle *EFG*? Round to the nearest tenth.

b. Is the triangle equilateral, isosceles, or scalene?

8. Higher Order Thinking There are points on a grid at (0, 0) and (3, 0).

a. What is a possible coordinate of the third vertex if the triangle has a perimeter of 11 units? Explain.

b. Is there another point that could be the third vertex? Explain.

☑ Assessment Practice

9. Find the distance, in units, between *P* and *Q*. Round to the nearest tenth.

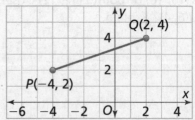

10. Find the distance, in units, between *S*(2.3, 4.8) and *T*(6.4, 7.9). Round to the nearest tenth.

13-1 Additional Practice

1. What is the surface area of the cylinder? Use 3.14 for π, and round to the nearest tenth.

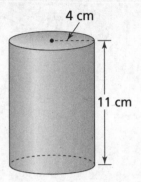

4 cm

11 cm

2. What is the surface area of the ball shown? Use $\frac{22}{7}$ for π, and round to the nearest whole number.

Radius is 9 centimeters.

3. The length of the radius and slant height of two different cones are shown.

   a. Find the surface area of each cone. Use 3.14 for π, and round to the nearest hundredth.

   b. Which cone has the greater surface area?

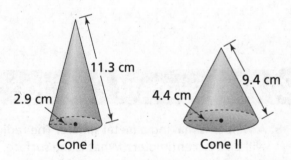

11.3 cm

2.9 cm

9.4 cm

4.4 cm

Cone I   Cone II

4. A sphere has a surface area of 9,244 square feet.

   a. What is the radius of the sphere? Use 3.14 for π, and round to the nearest hundredth.

   b. Make Sense and Persevere How can you check your answer?

5. Sergio works at a bakery and needs to cover eight identical cylindrical cakes with frosting. The bottom of each cake does not need frosting. What surface area of each cake needs to be frosted? Use 3.14 for π, and round to the nearest hundredth.

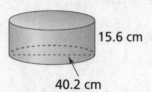

15.6 cm

40.2 cm

6. What is the surface area of the cone? Use 3.14 for π, and round to the nearest whole number.

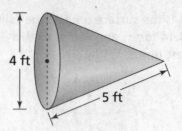

4 ft

5 ft

7. Higher Order Thinking A cylindrical vase has height 17 inches and radius 3 inches.

a. Find the exact surface area of the vase in terms of π.

b. Suppose a second vase has double the radius, but the same surface area. What is the height of the vase?

☑ Assessment Practice

8. A welder is making a metal sphere. The radius will be 115 centimeters. What is the surface area of the metal sphere? Use 3.14 for π.

Ⓐ About 166,106 cm²

Ⓑ About 52,900 cm²

Ⓒ About 664,424 cm²

Ⓓ About 41,526.5 cm²

9. Thirty percent of the metal sphere from Exercise 8 will be covered in a metal that is tinted red. What is the area, to the nearest square centimeter, of the tinted section of the sphere?

13-2 Additional Practice

1. Leveled Practice What is the volume of the cylinder? Use 3.14 for π.

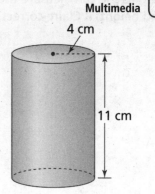

4 cm

11 cm

$V = \pi \cdot \boxed{}^2 \cdot \boxed{}$

$= \pi \cdot \boxed{} \cdot \boxed{}$

$= \boxed{}\,\pi$

The volume of the cylinder is about $\boxed{}$ cubic centimeters.

2. The volume of the cylinder is 48π cubic feet. The area of the base is 12π square feet. What is the height of the cylinder?

3. You are building a sand castle and want to use a cylindrical bucket that holds 885 cubic inches of sand. If the bucket has a height of 11.7 inches, what is the radius of the bucket? Use 3.14 for π, and round to the nearest tenth.

4. A cylinder has radius 2.3 inches and height 5.5 inches.

2.3 in.

5.5 in.

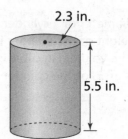

a. Find the volume of the cylinder. Use 3.14 for π, and round to the nearest tenth.

b. Reasoning If the radius of the cylinder is changed, but the height remains the same, how will the volume change?

5. **Critique Reasoning** Claire says that she can find the volume of any cylinder as long as she can measure the circumference and height. Is Claire correct? Explain.

6. Find the volume of each cylinder in terms of π. Which cylinder has the greatest volume?

   Cylinder A: diameter = 7 in., height = 12 in.

   Cylinder B: diameter = 12 in., height = 7 in.

7. **Higher Order Thinking** The cylinder shown is a steel tube that weighs 0.2835 pound per cubic inch. The inner part of the tube is hollow. What is the weight of the tube? Use 3.14 for π, and round to the nearest tenth.

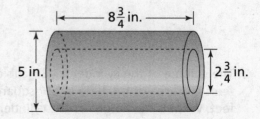

8$\frac{3}{4}$ in.

5 in.

2$\frac{3}{4}$ in.

8. The diameter of a cylinder is $(6x - 8)$ in. and the height of the cylinder is $(11x + 10)$ in. Find the volume, in cubic inches and in terms of π, of the cylinder when $x = 7$.

9. The volume of a cylinder is $4{,}000\pi$ in.^{3}. The height of the cylinder is 250 in. What is the radius, in inches, of the cylinder?

13-3 Additional Practice

Leveled Practice In **1** and **2**, find the volume of each cone.

1. What is the volume of the cone? Use 3.14 for π.

$V \approx \frac{1}{3}(3.14)()^2()$

$V = \frac{1}{3}(3.14)()()$

$V = \frac{1}{3}()$

$V = $ units^3

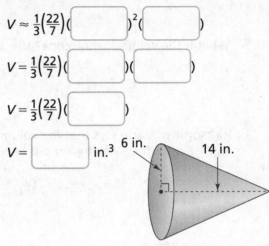

45

20

2. Find the volume of the cone. Use $\frac{22}{7}$ for π.

$V \approx \frac{1}{3}\left(\frac{22}{7}\right)()^2()$

$V = \frac{1}{3}\left(\frac{22}{7}\right)()()$

$V = \frac{1}{3}\left(\frac{22}{7}\right)()$

$V = $ in.^{3}

6 in.   14 in.

3. A trap to catch fruit flies uses a cone in a jar. The cone is shown.

a. What is the volume of the cone? Write your answer in terms of π.

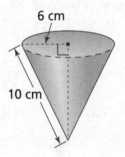

6 cm

10 cm

b. Reasoning Explain why an answer in terms of π is more accurate than an answer that uses 3.14 for π.

4. An artist makes a small cone-shaped sculpture for his class. The circumference of the sculpture is 3.14 feet. What is the volume of the sculpture? Use 3.14 for π.

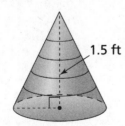

1.5 ft

5. The cone has a volume of 15,225π cubic millimeters. What is the radius of the base?

203 mm

6. The volume of a cone is 763.02 cubic inches. The radius and height of the cone are equal. What is the radius of the cone? Use 3.14 for π.

7. What is the volume of the cone? Use 3.14 for π.

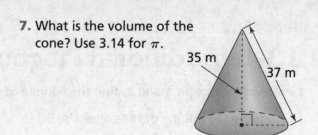

35 m

37 m

8. a. What is the volume of the cone? Use 3.14 for π.

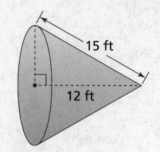

15 ft

12 ft

b. Reasoning Mario says that the volume of the cone is 1,271.7 cubic feet. What error did he likely make?

9. A cone has a height of 14 centimeters and a base with a circumference of 8.4π centimeters. What is the volume of the cone in terms of π?

10. Higher Order Thinking A cone has a radius of 39 centimeters and a slant height of 65 centimeters.

a. What is the volume of the cone in terms of π?

b. Reasoning If the radius is now half the size and the height is the same, how has the volume of the cone changed?

☑ Assessment Practice

11. List the cones described below in order from least volume to greatest volume.

- Cone 1: radius 16 cm and height 12 cm
- Cone 2: radius 12 cm and height 16 cm
- Cone 3: radius 8 cm and height 24 cm

Ⓐ Cone 1, Cone 2, Cone 3

Ⓑ Cone 2, Cone 1, Cone 3

Ⓒ Cone 3, Cone 2, Cone 1

Ⓓ Cone 3, Cone 1, Cone 2

12. What is the volume, in cubic inches, of a cone that has a radius of 9 inches and a height of 16 inches? Use 3.14 for π, and round to the nearest hundredth.

PRACTICE   TUTORIAL

13-4 Additional Practice

Scan for
Multimedia

1. Leveled Practice A solid plastic sphere has a radius of 8 inches. How much plastic does it take to make one sphere? Use 3.14 for π, and round to the nearest whole number.

Use the formula $V = \frac{4}{3}\pi r^3$.

$$V = \frac{4}{3}\pi(\boxed{}^3)$$

$$V = \frac{4}{3}\pi(\boxed{})$$

$$V \approx \frac{4}{3}(\boxed{})(\boxed{})$$

$$V \approx (\boxed{})$$

It takes approximately $\boxed{}$ cubic inches of plastic to make one sphere.

2. A sphere has a diameter of 0.926 inch.

   a. What is the volume of the sphere? Use 3.14 for π, and round to the nearest thousandth.

   b. Reasoning How does the volume of this sphere compare to the volume of a sphere with radius 0.926 inch?

3. Find the volume of the figure. Use 3.14 for π, and round to the nearest whole number.

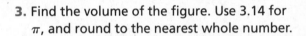
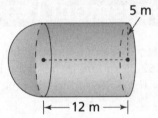

5 m

|← 12 m →|

4. A spherical container has surface area of about 5,538.96 square centimeters.

   a. What is the volume of the container? Use 3.14 for π, and round to the nearest hudredth.

   b. Make Sense and Persevere If 600 cubic centimeters of water flow into the container in one minute, about how many minutes will it take to fill the container?

5. A sphere has a radius of 19 inches.

    a. What is the volume of the sphere? Use 3.14 for π, and round to the nearest hundredth.

    b. Describe how the volume of the sphere changes if the radius is increased by 1.

6. Higher Order Thinking Find the volume of the solid where the two hemispheres are hollow. Explain. Use 3.14 for π, and round to the nearest hundredth.

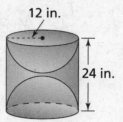

Assessment Practice

7. The surface area of a globe in Mr. Patton's classroom is about 452.39 square inches. Find its volume in cubic inches. Use 3.14 for π. Round to the nearest whole number.

8. A septic tank has the shape shown. How many gallons of fluid does it hold? Use 3.14 for π, and round to the nearest gallon. Note: $1 \text{ ft}^3 \approx 7.48$ gal.

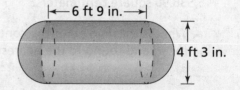